Wrestle for the Border town

Berwick

Berwick

How the fight started...

...and continues to this day.

By Kevin Scott

Bellendain Books
Scotland

Copyright © 2019 by Kevin Scott

All rights reserved. This book or any portion thereof may not be reproduced or used in any manner whatsoever without the express written permission of the publisher except for the use of brief quotations in a book review or scholarly journal.

First Printing: 2019

ISBN: 978-0-244-17445-3

Bellendain Books

SCOTLAND

Berwick

How the fight started....
....and continues to this day.

Berwick (upon Tweed) is one of Britain's most historic towns, picturesquely situated at the northern apex of Northumberland, presenting a striking appearance sitting astride a multi-bridged river, though the bulk of it sits on, what was once called, the Scottish bank of the River Tweed.

No other town in North-East England has had a more eventful history than Berwick. There is no doubt that it can claim the distinction of being a border town, as it has changed hands between England and Scotland, officially, no less than twenty-one times. Its history is inextricably tied up with the struggle for the Anglo-Scottish frontier, Berwick , itself, now lying some 2.5 miles(4km) south of the Scottish border !

ENGLISH OR SCOTTISH ?

Today, a visitor to Berwick can be forgiven for believing it to be a Scottish town as, after all, it stands on the northern bank of the River Tweed, an entirely Scottish river and it does seem to have a rather Scottish appearance. Berwick's River Tweed, is officially recognised as Scottish and may not be fished on a Sunday (unlike English rivers),whilst Berwick was also the name of a large Scottish Burgh and the old county of Berwickshire (of which Berwick is now not part) is in Scotland.

Furthermore, Berwick is a little bit closer to the Scottish capital of Edinburgh, than to the North East's regional centre of Newcastle upon Tyne. Berwick is advertised by English Tourism as A "Gateway to Scotland", whilst it also features in online sites as somewhere to visit in "Undiscovered Scotland!. So too the road signs, with visitors being greeted on the A1 with "Welcome to Scotland" heading north whilst, a rather more hesitant, "Welcome to Northumberland" greets the traveller heading south.

The belief that Berwick is Scottish is also reinforced by the fact that most of the commercial banks in the town are Scottish and that the local football team plays in the Scottish league, as does its rugby team. There are Scottish building societies, and there is the Berwickshire Sports Council, Berwickshire Housing Association and even a local newspaper, The Berwickshire News, all based in the town. So too has one of the Middle schools, its very own tartan, whilst local restaurants and butchers, in the town centre, sell haggis alongside the roast beef, with the Town Hall annually hosting its own St Andrews Day celebrations every November 30th!

The Berwickshire News

Dialect also leads us to the belief that Berwick is Scottish as, to most Englishmen, the local 'Tweedside' accent, spoken in Berwick, sounds more lowland Scottish, although most Scots would recognise its Northumbrian influence. Border Television covers Berwick from Carlisle, whilst the local Radio Borders is transmitted from Melrose, itself well inside the Scottish Borders.

The red sandstone of Berwick's buildings, too, have a characteristic Scottish look to them, in an area of Britain, its own town council readily now concedes as " an area considered too far north for England"!

The Scottish claim for Berwick is, therefore, certainly strong but the English influence upon the area is also very significant. Berwick, as we shall soon see, began as an English or, at least, an Anglo-Saxon settlement, in the Kingdom of Northumbria and although, for four hundred years, it would regularly change hands between England and Scotland, it has remained in the former part of the United Kingdom for the past five centuries. Berwick's policemen and laws are therefore English, and its most senior councillor is an English mayor, not a provost as in the Scottish system of local government, and yet the bearer wears robes of purple, and not scarlet, as they would have been in the days when the town was a royal Scottish burgh!

The Romans had built Hadrian's Wall, between Brittania (roughly modern England and Wales) and Caledonia (modern Scotland), primarily, to protect its Empire from the more lawless of the Scottish tribes. The borderline, then, was to follow the Cheviot range of mountains, which ran across southern Scotland and northern England, to then join with the easterly course of the River Tweed which flowed into its estuary at Tweedmouth, on the English side, or Berwick , as was, on the Scottish side.

Founded during the time of the kingdom of Northumbria, the area would become central to historic border wars, fought between the kingdoms of Scotland and England for centuries. Until the Union of the Crowns in 1707, the region on either side of the boundary would become a lawless territory, suffering from the repeated raids, in each direction, of the border raiders, or "reivers" whose domain then became known as "the Debateable Lands."

But let's rewind to some of Berwick's beginnings, if we can, to try and establish its original ownership.

Anglo-Saxon Origins

Early history shows us that, in the post-Roman period, the border area may have been inhabited by the Brythons of Bryneich, who were in turn conquered by the Angles, who were then to create the kingdom of Bernicia, which would then unite with the kingdom of Deira, to form what is now known simply as Northumbria.

For much of the 7th and 8th Centuries, the Christian kingdom of Northumbria then extended from the River Humber, stretching northwards to the Firth of Forth, at Edinburgh. Its royal capital was at Bamburgh, some 20 miles south along the coast from Berwick.

Berwick

Bamburgh's fortress rock is still visible from Berwick's ramparts today, but it was during this Anglo-Saxon period that a township began to grow up at the mouth of the River Tweed at a place called Bere-wic, or "Barley/corn -farm". Other writers claim the name stems from Aber-wick, the town at the mouth of a river, or, even, the Norse "vik"(meaning bay) and bar (headland), which cuts across the Tweed estuary here. Berwick was then referred to as South Berwick by the Scots, to differentiate it from the town of North Berwick in East Lothian, east of Edinburgh, the later nation's capital city.

It is thought that Berwick's bridge which spanned the river here, even in pre-Roman times, and was to be successively repaired by the Romans, Saxons and Danes ,was the precursor to many future spans between the two warring countries of Scotland and England, before finally ending with the Royal Border Bridge being completed in 1850.Built by railway pioneer Robert Stephenson and opened by Queen Victoria, its viaduct with 28 magnificent arches, strides gracefully across the River Tweed, and is still in regular use today as part of the main Newcastle-Edinburgh ,East Coast, railway main line.

Peter Langtoft, also known as Peter of Langtoft, (died c. 1305) was an English historian and chronicler, as well as an Augustinian monk at Bridlington Priory, who wrote a histo-

Berwick

ry of England in Anglo-Norman verse, popularly known as *Langtoft's Chronicle*. The history narrated the history of England from the legendary founding of Britain, by Brutus, to the death of King Edward1st. On the whole, the Chronicle is, virulently, anti-Scottish and famously contains nine 'songs', in both Anglo-Norman and Middle English, supposedly capturing the taunts between English and Scottish soldiers during the Anglo-Scottish conflicts of the late-13th and early-14th centuries. Fair to say, then, that there would have been no bias in reporting any Scottish advantages at this time. However, in Langtoft's Chronicle' the following lines occur:

"In ye zere after [833] right in the time of May,
(In the year after AD 833)
Oseth, ye Danes Kyng, com Inglond to affraie.
(Oseth, the Danish king came to England to fight)
He aryved at Berwick, in the water of Twede,
(He arrived at the mouth of the River Tweed)
Priue help of ye Scottes he had at his nede
(praying for the help of the Scots, he needed)
And com fast toward ye South grete powere he led."
(he led his great army south to England)

Kevin Scott

The territory of Lothian, what is today South-East Scotland, between the rivers Tweed and Forth, had been part of the northern kingdom of Northumbria from the mid-seventh century until that fateful year of 867, when the Danes conquered York and established their own kingdom of Jorvik. Around 872, (first mention of Berwick in the Chronicles) a Pictish king Grig, or Gregory, swept down upon Northumbria, gaining possession of Bamburgh and laying waste to the holy island of Lindisfarne. He was also recorded as wintering in Berwick but, cut off from their fellow English, they were unable to resist pressure from the North where the Kings of Scotland were, by now, pursuing their own territorial ambitions southwards. By 962, the Scots had captured Edinburgh and much of Lothian had fallen under the sway of these new kings of the north. With the loss of Lothian, the Lords of Bamburgh were now keener to retain the southern half of their domain. Many say that the Scots gained Lothian as a result of the battle, forgetting that Malcolm 11(prior to becoming King of Scotland himself in 1005) was still paying homage to the English King Edgar for his having ceded the lands of Lothian in 973!

Berwick

Records do show that Berwick was formally granted to the Scottish King Kenneth 11, by Edgar "The Pacific", King of England.

Malcolm 11 became King in 1005 and, after suffering a defeat at Durham in 1006, and vowing to avenge this most handsomely, he duly did in 1018 (or possibly1016), at the Battle of Carham (on Tweed), a hamlet just southwest of Coldstream, a few miles upstream from Berwick. It was even sometimes referred to as the Battle of Coldstream.

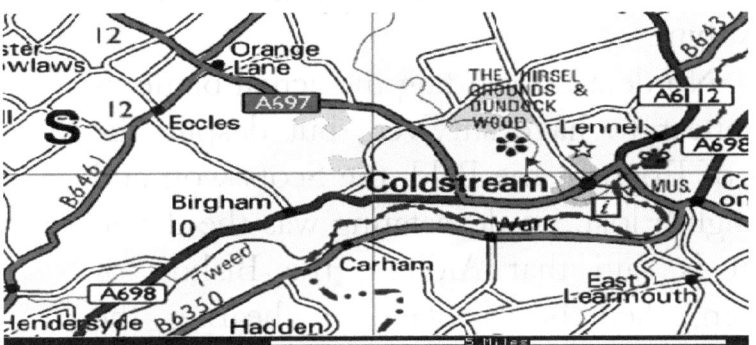

On one side was Malcolm11, King of the Scots and , with the support of his ally, Eoghain (Owain) the Bald ,the King of Strathclyde, was to take advantage of the absence of the reigning King Cnut, (Canute), who was in Denmark, to press his claims for sovereignty over the Lordship of Bamburgh, (and probably hoping that victory might being with it an opportunity to recover Lothian).

When Eardulph-Cudel, the slow and sluggish prince, who ruled over the Northumbrian earldom, met in pitched battle, with all his forces, who it is said, he had levied all Northumbrian men, North of the River Tees and South of Tweed, in order to resist the invasion, again implying that Scotland's border was once more down at Berwick! However, King Malcolm was anxious to extend the southern limits of his kingdom, and he routed the massed, southern forces hastily gathered against him.

No details regarding the actual battle itself appear to have survived, but despite the death of Eoghain the Bald, the Scots won and the English lost. So devastating was the defeat that it is said that Aldhun, the Bishop of Durham, died heartbroken on hearing the news, hoping that Cnut's efforts to establish himself as the future ruler of all England, after defending Northumbria, would have continued. Eadulf Cudel died in 1019, probably at the hands of King Cnut as punishment for his failure.

Simeon of Durham wrote that 'all the people who dwelt between Tees and Tweed were, now, well-nigh exterminated'. It meant a significant shift in the balance of power in the North, then confirming Scotland's hold on Lothian, and helping to establish the Tweed as the border. King Malcolm now claimed the Tweed as a Scottish river and Berwick as being a town within the boundary of Scotia, this area of Northumbria, to the north of Tweed, now being totally ceded to the Scots.

But despite being a great victory for the Scots, Malcolm did not achieve his objective, as the territory of the Lordship of Bamburgh still remained outside his grasp. Malcolm does not seem to have followed up his victory with any further move southwards; quite why, no one knows, perhaps the victory was somewhat pyrrhic and he lacked the military resources to press home his advantage. In 1029 Canute, King of England, Denmark and Norway, invaded Scotland and seems to have recognised Malcolm's possession of Lothian. This could be recognition of the "de facto" occupation of Lothian by the Scots before 973. As Barrow says, 'What English annalists recorded as the 'cession' of Lothian, was the recognition by a powerful but extremely remote south-country king of a long-agreed territory."

The Battle of Carham was really only part of the process that severed Lothian from its centuries old connection with England and would lead to the development of the new nation, called Scotland. In 1031 Canute/Cnut, the Danish King of England, came north, and demanded homage from Malcolm for the recently annexed part of Scotland. This homage was performed by the northern King in due form. Previous to this time Bernicia had extended to the Forth, and Bamborough was the royal town of this extensive territory. Berwick was not

Berwick

much noted before the period preceding 1030. A mere village it must have been, neither a boundary town nor a fortified place; for Bamborough, only some 20 miles south of Berwick, would not have suffered such a stronghold in its immediate neighbourhood, especially on the opposite side of such an important river. When the River Tweed would, at length, become the dividing-line of the two kingdoms, and Berwick became the border town to defend that line, it was only natural that Berwick should, at once, leap into greatness, and a rudely fortified castle assumed shape, on that knoll to the north-west of the town, which would for ages become one of the most historically noted places in our country, (Scotland, that is).

To support this view, in the text of the origin of Berwick's rapid prosperity, the following details are given by Skene in his 'Celtic Scotland': "The Kings of Scotland had now become possessors of conquered territory; the Lothians were now their own; and what more likely than that, they should attempt to extend their limits still further south, and make the Tyne, instead of the Tweed, their southern boundary?

Duncan, grandson of King Malcolm 11, fired with this ambition, determined, shortly after 1030 , upon a trial of strength with his southern foes. He easily overran the northern part, penetrating the land till he threatened Durham. Here his further progress was stayed as he met the English force, resulting in a punitive expedition being launched northwards in the years 1030-1031, where he was defeated and, for a while, the Scots would be persuaded to modify their ambitions. His army was put to a disorderly flight, in which all his foot soldiers were lost and numbers of his cavalry slain. Duncan was thus compelled to retreat with his self-imposed task unfulfilled. On arriving at Berwick, where he was met by Moddan, an Earl whom he had appointed ruler over Orkney and Caithness, he learned that this earldom had been seized by Thorfinn, his own cousin, and son of Sigurd, late Earl of the Orkneys. Duncan determined to proceed northwards in person to Moddan's assistance. The latter set out at once by land; but the King fitted out, at Berwick, a fleet of eleven war-ships, and set sail

Berwick

on the fatal expedition, which would end very shortly afterwards in his assassination by Macbeth, of Shakespearian renown.

King Duncan was assassinated in 1040, his young son Malcolm then being sent to England for safety, because he was nearly related to Siward the Dane, who was at that time Earl of Northumberland. Macbeth, the usurper, now ruled over Scotland for seventeen years. He had sufficient to do with his own turbulent people, to keep him from molesting the English. In 1054, when Malcolm was of age to think about regaining his hereditary throne, he, with the aid of Siward, then penetrated to the heart of Scotland, by both land and sea, to try and conquer his rival. In this expedition, as in Duncan's, Berwick would be the starting-place from where to sail into Scotland. The expedition, thus begun, terminated in desperate fighting, and in partial defeat of Macbeth, Malcolm being consequently installed King of Cumbria and Lothian, over which he would rule for the next thirty-five years.

Berwick

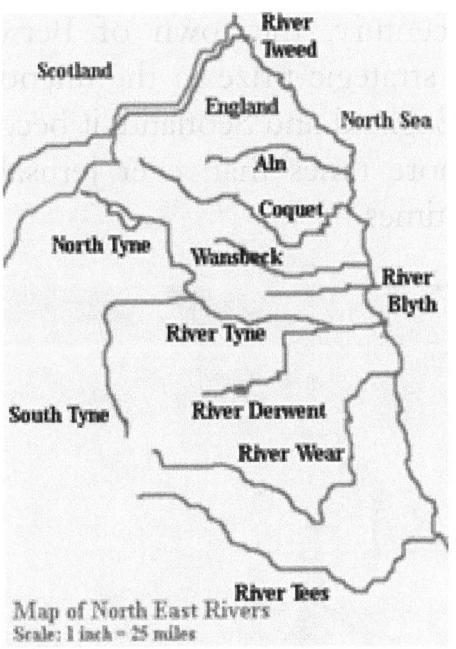

Map of North East Rivers
Scale: 1 inch = 25 miles

Safe now in his own territory, he harried after the usual fashion, making repeated inroads into Northumbria, but, at length, being compelled to come to terms by William the Conqueror, the then King of England. When King Rufus began his reign, Malcolm again resumed his predatory habits, and entered Northumberland with the old idea of extending his border-line down to the River Tyne. A peace was again concluded, in which Malcolm owned and acknowledged Rufus's overlordship of the Lothians. Malcolm 111, Macbeth, Duncan 11 & Donald 111 were all then made subsequent kings of Scotland until 1097. From the mid-11th century, the town of Berwick then became a strategic prize in the unending wars between England and Scotland, it becoming besieged more times than ever Jerusalem was, at least 14 times.

Canmore died in 1093 and, for four years after this, the Scottish throne was given up to the conflicting claims of different aspirants. Towards the close of this period a successful attempt was made to place Eadgar, son of Malcolm, in kingly power. In this he was assisted by an army sent from England. Fordun, in his "Chronicles", said that while Eadgar was going North, St. Cuthbert appeared to him in a dream, and advised him to carry his (Cuthbert's) standard from Durham in front of his army, which would be sure to bring him "victory and success"(Berwick's motto today).

He Eadgar then founded anew the Monastery of Coldingham in 1097 ; and "this princely man", adds Fordun, "heaped gift upon gift, and would confirm(confer) also, by gift, to the Bishop of Durham and his successors, the noble village of Berwick, with all its appurtenances"(belongings). We believe this to be the earliest indisputable notice of the town of Berwick, in King Edgar's charter. The same statement is referred to in the Trinity College Library, Cambridge, the handwriting of which belongs to the first half of the twelfth century. In this it is said that King Eadgar gave Berwick to St. Cuthbert, with all its belongings but would revoke the gift soon afterwards. The same matter is referred to in a greatly disputed charter of Eadgar's, a charter whose authenticity is believed in by Raine but denied by Skene. This gift is said, by historians, to have been made to Ralph Flambard, Bishop of Durham, who is said to have shortly afterwards assaulted one of Eadgar's favourite captains, hence the King revoking the gift so quickly from so ungrateful a recipient.

The rest of Eadgar's reign passed in peace. He died in 1107, and was succeeded by his brother Alexander the Fierce who would rule over the north of Scotland, and by David, his younger brother, who would rule over the southern parts of the country, ie. the Lothians and Cumbria, 17 years before his becoming David 1 King of Scotland from 1124 until 1153,a long and most beneficial reign for the people.

Berwick

The Bishop of St Andrews, at this time, was erecting a burgh and Berwick was approached for the teaching of its citizens, the customs and usages of a burgh. In the 11th Century, the fishing port of Berwick was sufficiently large enough to now harbour over a dozen war vessels of the Scottish king.

In the history of the country, during all this time, we do not find any reference to Berwick, or its inhabitants of that day, taking part with the King, in his foreign or domestic raids, against his enemies. His transactions with his neighbours in Northumberland were important, but throw little or no light upon the town's history. Alexander 1 had become King of Scotland in 1107 and ,in 1120, was to make Berwick-upon-Tweed one of Scotland's four Royal "Burghs" (note Scottish spelling),thus allowing the town's freemen a number of valuable rights and privileges that would allow the town to prosper and become Scotland's greatest seaport, and also its largest and wealthiest town by the 13th century.

One of the most wealthy trading ports in Scotland, Berwick thrived on the export of wool, grain and salmon, and traders from Germany, Holland and Flanders, the Low Countries, set up their homes and businesses in the town to turn it into a major international commercial centre, so populous and of such commercial importance, as it was described by one medieval writer as the new "Alexandria of the North". (They also brought with them their distinctive red pan-tiled roofing , still very prevalent today in the town ,and indeed up much of Scotland's eastern coastline. Berwick now provided an annual customs value of £2,190, then equivalent to a quarter of all customs revenues received north of the border, directly into the Scottish Exchequer. The customs of the whole of England were only four times as large!

Apart from making Berwick a Royal Burgh, King David also began establishing new monastaries in Scotland and further promoted trade by standardising weights and measures and also starting royal mints, the one built at Berwick producing Scottish coinage.

Some scribes chronicled David as having gained the Scottish throne largely because of the support of Henry 1 of England, and that he was attempting to remodel Scotland to be more like Henry's England. He had carried out peaceful changes in the areas of Scotland, over which he had effective control, and had conducted military campaigns against semi-autonomous regional rulers to reassert his authority; whilst in administration, warfare, and in the settling of regained territory, he had drawn on the talent and resources of the Anglo-Norman lands. The death of Henry I in 1135, weakening England, made David more reliant on his native subjects, and allowed him to contemplate winning control over substantial areas of northern England.

In spring 1137, David again invaded England, though a truce was quickly agreed. In November, the truce expired and now David demanded to be made Earl of the whole of the old Earldom of Northumberland. King Stephen, of England, refused and in January 1138 David invaded for a third time.

Advancing beyond the River Tees towards York, early on 22 August 1138, the Scots found the English army drawn up on open fields two miles north of Northallerton, south of the Tyne. They were to be routed by much superior "Norman" weaponry and armour, which resulted in an estimated 10,000 of King David's army being slewn in battle and in flight. Despite losing this battle (of the Standard), David was subsequently given most of the territorial concessions he had been seeking (which many of the Chronicles actually say he had been offered even before he had crossed the Tees). David held these till his death but, his successor, Malcolm IV of Scotland, was soon forced to surrender David's gains to Henry II of England.

Kevin Scott

Negotiations between Kings David, of Scotland, and Stephen of England continued over the winter months until, on April 9, David's son, Henry, and Stephen's wife, Mathilda of Boulogne, met each other at Durham and agreed a settlement,(Treaty of Durham).

Henry was given the earldom of Northumberland and was restored to the Earldom of Huntingdon and Lordship of Doncaster whilst David, himself, was allowed to keep Carlisle and Cumberland. However, King Stephen was to retain possession of the strategically vital castles of Bamburgh and Newcastle, and Prince Henry was to perform homage for his English lands, while David was to promise to "remain loyal" to Stephen at all times. This arrangement lasted for nearly 20 years, and would appear to have been beneficial to both sides. David was able to benefit from the resources of Northern England (for example, the lead mines of the northern Pennines giving him silver, from which he was able to strike his own coinage).

The new, southern, border of David's realm appeared to be permanently secured in 1149, when Matilda's son, Henry, was knighted by David at Carlisle, he having first given an oath that, if he became king of England, he would give to David, Newcastle and all Northumbria, and would permit him and his heirs to possess in peace, without counter-claim forever, the whole land which lay from the Rivers Tweed to Tyne!

Berwick Castle was built in 1150 and, by 1167, we read of William the Lion, King of Scotland (crowned 1165) then imprisoning people within its walls. During his reign, Scotland would prosper greatly. Wool, fish and furs were exported whilst luxuries such as wine and spices were imported through the seaport of Berwick.

Berwick

King Henry 11 of England's high handed approach caused a number of barons to throw off their allegiance to their king. The King's eldest son, Henry, who had been crowned in the early part of his father's reign, was urged by the Queen to rebel and demand from his father the realm over which he had been crowned. By large promises , he attached the barons to his side, and in like manner he gained over the King of Scots by promising him both Northumberland and Cumberland.

William, on his part, was to invade England and assist the disloyal English to establish the young Henry on the throne. King William1" the Lion"of Scotland, was to continuously invade Northumbria and, in carrying out this programme, laid siege to Carlisle and generally ravaged right across the northern counties. On King William's withdrawal to Berwick, he would then be followed by the English Justiciar Richard de Lucy and the Constable, Humphrey de Bohun, before whom he fled back into Scotland. These English leaders brought their army across the Tweed, burnt Berwick, and its castle, and laid waste the surrounding country.

This is the first instance of a long series of disasters which we have to chronicle about Berwick:

Henry-de-Bohun, who boldly advances" caused to the King, the loss of Berwick. Lord Humphrey-de-Bohun was of very great consequence as the Barons of Northumberland were his companions. "They burnt all Berwick with fire and firebrands in it, and a great part of the surrounding country".

Berwick was not long in recovering this damage. Wooden houses soon blaze to the ground and are quickly restored, so the calamity, terrible in its swift retribution, would soon be forgotten, and Berwick would return in a short time to its career of prosperity. Disturbances of a serious nature had then recalled the English army southwards. The Lion King sought to assist, in another expedition, the re-

Berwick

bel son of the English King and, under his protection, penetrated with an army right into England. However, driven back a second time by an English southern force, William was slowly retiring towards Scotland, when he was surprised, ambushed and captured at Alnwick by Randulph de Glanville, Justiciar. This terrible misfortune told heavily upon Scotland for a time as William was carried to Northampton, to the King's presence, with all the indignity of a captive but, before the end of the same year (1174), he would have bought his liberty and freedom by then recognising Henry 11 as his feudal lord, and doing homage for his whole kingdom.

The Treaty of Falaise arranged the terms of William's surrender and, to ensure a proper observance or surety of the terms of the treaty, the English King then demanded five of William's Scottish castles to be given up to his keeping. Berwick Castle was one of these, where it would now remain for fifteen years in the hands of the English. This is the second mention of Berwick Castle that can be relied upon. It could not be of any great age at this time, nor is it at all probable that it was a castle of any strength, for Burton says that 'down to the opening of the War of Independence, there were very few castles built of stone in Scotland.' But, if we must credit Camden, Henry II. rebuilt the castle while it was subject to English rule. If he did so, he would now change the rude fort into a well-fortified place, and at least lay the foundation of that structure that was in all its glory of unassailable strength during the reigns of the following three King Edwards. The castle was now governed by the English, and garrisoned by English soldiers. Many have said that Berwick was only ever seen by the English as a garrison frontier and never really regarded, then or now, as a main city, unlike Scotland.

Berwick

Scotland complained bitterly about their being forced to surrender and hand over Berwick to the English as part of their king's ransom, some 10,000 merks, (£8000 in today's money), but the English claim to Scotland, they said, went back much further than this formal act of submission.

Berwick then remained relatively peaceful for the next 15 years until 1189, when the incumbent King of England, King Richard 1,(1189-1199), sold the homage of the Scottish king, and Berwick, back to Scotland to raise money for the Crusades. The amount of 10,000 merks for both Berwick and Edinburgh Castles was made to enable their returns to the northern side of the border, again free from English bondage. For we are told that Richard, King of England, has restored to his dearest cousin William, King of Scotland, his castles of Roxburgh and Berwick as his own, by hereditary right ! During the rest of Richard's reign there was profound peace between the two countries, and Berwick, as usual, drops out of sight in world history.

However, upon King John's ascension to the English throne in 1199, King William began, again, to assert his claims to both Northumberland and Westmoreland. Negotiations, with this end in view, proceeded very slowly. King John's design was to secure an open road to Scotland, and the Lion King's determination was to allow of no such highway, nor any defence erected for that purpose.King John continued for some years in no amiable mood at William's destructive conduct, until at length, in 1209, a treaty was framed at Norham Castle, in which John undertook never again to attempt this towerbuilding, and William on his part gave his two daughters to be married to the two sons of the English King,promising also to pay 1,000 marks ,in consideration of these marriages, for the damage done in demolishing the King John's works at Tweedmouth ; and thus, in a grumbling, half-satisfied spirit, both Kings maintained their peace until the close of William's reign.

Berwick

After Alexander 11 became Scottish King in 1214, he had lain siege to Norham Castle, south of Tweed which, incensing the English King John,(Richard's brother) then led an army north, on the 15th of January,1216, to retake Berwick town and the rebuilt castle, destroying not only the Tweed Bridge and burning Berwick and Coldingham as punishment, but also perpetrating the most horrible cruelties upon its citizens. King John himself, it was reported, attended in person the razing of the town with some barbarity. John travelled as far as Haddington, and, on returning, he plundered Coldingham and burnt Berwick in a most shameful manner, setting fire with his own hand to the house he had slept in that night, 'contra morem regem indecenter.'

This destructive raid of John's led only to reprisals. He had no sooner gone south, called thither by the turbulence of his own barons, than Alexander ravaged Northumberland and Cumberland in a most cruel manner. On 1st December 1217, King Alexander of Scotland's, sentence of excommunication was cancelled by the Pope, with the king receiving his absolution in the Berwick Castle.

The kingdoms now enjoyed a period of tranquillity. The Scottish King ceased from this time to make demands on the English King for part of his territory, and the Borders were, temporarily, at rest. An attempt was now made to trace out the boundary line between England and Scotland, which ended in both parties, leaving for centuries, a part called the ' debateable lands,' which could be assigned to neither country.

Berwick

While external peace thus prevailed, the countries became prosperous. Trade, home and foreign, was developed in no ordinary degree. The terribly destructive raids of William the Lion must have checked the trade of Berwick in its natural increase but, during the reigns of the two Alexanders, the town developed rapidly. Its exports, in particular, grew to vast importance. Before David I.'s time, Fordun called it the noble village of Berwick as did William of Newbury too, in the twelfth century, again refer to it as the noble town of Berwick, belonging to the King of Scots. The 'Lanercost Chronicle', about the middle of this thirteenth century, now said that "this town was formerly so populous and of such commercial consequence that it could deservedly be called a second Alexandria, whose riches was the sea and the water was its walls," so extensive was its commerce.

We now reach another pivotal time in Berwick's history and this would occur in 1237 with the signing of the Treaty of York, which legally set to establishing the Anglo-Scottish border-line, with the exception of a small area around Berwick, which would be later taken by England in 1482.The border now ran some 154km /96m between the Solway Firth in the west, to the River Tweed in the east. By the Treaty of York of 1237, Scotland renounced its rights to Cumberland, Westmorland and Northumberland, with the border between the two countries being agreed. The Treaty of York was an agreement, or peace treaty, between Henry 111 of England and Alexander11 of Scotland signed, at York, on 25 September 1237.

Berwick

It detailed the future status of several feudal properties and addressed other issues between the two kings, and indirectly marked the end of Scotland's attempts to extend its frontier southward, though it didn't address any issues of the future determination of the Anglo-Scottish border. The treaty was one of a number of agreements in the ongoing relationship between the two kings, Henry and Alexander, who had a history of making agreements to settle one matter or another, related to this, being their personal relationship in that Alexander was now married to Henry's sister, Joan.

The title of the agreement reached on 25 September and "respecting all claims, or competent to, the latter, up to Friday next before Michaelmas A.D. 1237", is *Scriptum cirographatum inter Henricum Regem Anglie et Alexandrum Regem Scocie de comitatu Northumbrie Cumbrie et Westmerland factum coram Ottone Legato* and the particulars of the agreement are:

The King of Scotland: quit claims to the King of England, his hereditary rights to the counties of Northumberland, Cumberland, and Westmorland; quit claims 15,000 marks of silver paid by King William to King John for certain conventions not observed by the latter;

and frees Henry from agreements regarding marriages between Henry and King Richard, and Alexander's sisters Margaret, Isabella, and Marjory.

The King of England grants the King of Scotland certain lands within Northumberland and Cumberland, to be held by him and his successor Kings of Scotland in feudal tenure with certain rights exempting them from obligations common in feudal relationships, and with the Scottish Steward sitting in Justice regarding certain issues that may arise, and these, too, are hereditary to the King of Scotland's heirs, and regarding these the King of Scotland shall not be answerable to an English court of law in any suit.

It is recorded that, in 1266, King Alexander of Scotland held his birthday celebrations in the town of Berwick, by then it being one of the wealthiest ports in Europe, earning a quarter of all Scottish customs revenues. In 1286 the customs of Berwick amounted to £2,190, annually paid into the Scottish Exchequer.

In the reign of Alexander 111(1247-1286, Berwick had now reached its highest point of prosperity.

For most of the thirteenth century, Scotland would retain much of its independence, being

Berwick

ruled by a strong, independent monarchy until 1286, when King Alexander III died.

Towards the close of Alexander III/s reign, facts disclose ,still more clearly, the greatness of Berwick's commerce in 1286.Goods were collected from the whole basin of the Tweed, where, in at that period, flourished the great monasteries of Melrose, Dryburgh, Jedburgh, and Kelso, attached to each being vast flocks of sheep and cattle. From all these Abbey-grounds, wools and skins were sent to the port of Berwick in large quantities. Northumberland sent its quota as well. In the town of Berwick was a colony of Flemings, assisting, to carry on and foster this trade. Their place of business was the Red Hall situated, according to tradition, in the street now called (not at all inappropriately) 'Woolmarket.' These Flemings, along with the native merchants, exported their goods to Flanders, and onwards to the markets in Bruges.

Berwick

Salmon formed part of the staple trade of the town, and were a considerable source of wealth to its inhabitants. We have mention made of minor trades—glovers, tanners, butchers, and bakers. Mills are also mentioned, and carefully regulated in their work. Brewers were plentiful, and the price of the ale was such that the commodity was within reach of all. The castle was fortified, and a great trade ensued in keeping it duly supplied with provisions for the King and his soldiers. We now see Berwick as a thriving Royal Burgh, with a port large enough to harbour a dozen of the Scottish Kings best fighting ships, whilst its trade steadily grew with European markets and prospered hugely, which would finally come to a climax in the reign of King Alexander the Third.

On reviewing the reigns of the kings from David's time, we find that they had all spent much time in Berwick. A house in the town was long known as the Palace, said to have been the residence of some of those early Kings. Charters are dated from Berwick in all these reigns. David was much about his royal town. The laws that were here framed, the Institution of the Court of the Royal Burghs, tell of much work. William the Lion in person repelled King John's attack at this place, and in addition to charters dated at Berwick in his reign, we must conclude that he saw much of the town and its neighbourhood. Alexander II dated three charters here in 1232, and had with him a large Court, consisting of the Abbot of Melrose, his Chancellor, Seneschal and Justiciar, Earl Patric, and his Chamberlain and in 1248, dating another charter here, just before his reign closed. So too did Alexander 111 spend a considerable part of his time in Berwick, most notably with his Queen before visiting with the English king, Henry 111. In 1266 the King of Scotland held his birthday regally, and with great rejoicing, in Berwick, with almost all the chief dependents of his kingdom, where were present Edmund, the younger son of the King of England, the Earl of Leicester, etc. In 1268 John, son of John Comyn, was knighted in Berwick by Alexander 111. He was the father of the Red John Comyn, who would be later slain by Robert the Bruce.

Berwick

In 1281 Alexander, for himself and his daughter Margaret, with the consent of his son and all his council, arranged with the ambassadors of Eric, King of Norway, for a marriage between the latter and Margaret, Alexander's daughter. Her marriage-portion was settled at 4,000 marks sterling. For at least one hundred years Scotland had been ruled by able kings, and latterly by kings peaceable as well, and Berwick had prospered during the calm but, in 1286, Alexander III's reign came to an abrupt close, through his violent death. He had been at a council meeting in Edinburgh on the 16th day of March, says Fordun, when he, after the meeting, had set out to proceed to Kinghorn, where his Queen, Joleta, was staying. He was delayed at Queensferry until it was dark and, not taking advice to stay at Inverkeithing that night, set out to ride in the dark along the coast of Fife, opposite to Edinburgh. Near the present burgh of Kinghorn he had to pass over a rugged promontory of basaltic rock. Stumbling, he was pitched over one of the rocks and killed. Such was the final calamity, opening one of the gloomiest chapters in the history of nations...

In 1290, Alexander's heir was his granddaughter, Margaret, daughter of the Norwegian king and queen who had since married the King of Norway, after his sale of Western Isles to Scotland in 1266. She, the "Maid of Nor-

Berwick

way", would not set out for Scotland for several years, and the country would be ruled in her absence by six Guardians, now appointed by the Scottish Parliament. Sailing from Norway, now mature enough, she unfortunately died on her voyage to Scotland and by so then leaving the country without a monarch, left the nobles to begin their arguing over the succession of the crown. Margaret's death in September 1290, on her way to Scotland, even threatened civil war breaking out between rival claimants for the vacant crown.

Here King Edward1, of England was an opportunist seeing his neighbouring Scots descent into civil war. The country was aligning itself between the two claimants to the throne: John Balliol, a descendent of Alexander III, with strong support from the Comyns in Dumfries , and to the north of the country; and Robert Bruce , who had support from the south, and from the Stewarts. Since Scotland was without a monarch, the Guardians' Seal had the Arms of Scotland on one side, and St Andrew on his saltire cross on the other, both of which were strong symbols of Scottish nationhood.

Kevin Scott

Berwick

The rule of the Guardians continued peacefully until 1290, when a marriage alliance was proposed between Margaret and Edward I's son, Edward of Caernarfon. A treaty of 1290 agreed the marriage and also bound England to preserve Scottish independence and the border agreed in 1237.

We now reach the year, 1291, when Edward 1 of England was then asked to arbitrate in the Scottish succession crisis and, at discussions at Norham in June 1291, he there demanded that the Guardians of Scotland, and the thirteen claimants to the Crown, duly acknowledge him as Superior Lord in Scotland. The Guardians were aware of the threat to Scotland's sovereignty, and despite reminding Edward that Scotland ruled her own affairs, they now underestimated his cunning. Edward found more candidates for the Scottish throne; there would have to be a legal judgement, and if he was presiding over the hearing, he would need the authority to do so.

John Balliol pays homage to Edward I of England

Berwick

The claimants were ambitious. First Bruce, then Balliol, paid homage to King Edward for, as judge, he was now controlling their destiny. Whoever was victorious had already surrendered Scotland's sovereignty, in lieu of their coronation.

An Assembly of the states of England and Scotland was held in Berwick Castle's Great Hall, where Edward 1 decided in favour of John Baliol, Lord of Galloway, against the claim of Robert the Bruce as heir to the Crown of Scotland. When, in 1292, Edward I gave Scotland to Balliol, eighty substantial burghers of Berwick also, similarly, took the same oath of allegiance to the English King Edward. Edward issued an order, on the 19th of

November, after sixteen months of discussion, for John Balliol to have seisin of the kingdom of Scotland; and another, commanding the castles of Scotland to be given to him. For this latter purpose he addressed Peter Burdett, the keeper of Berwick Castle, in these words:

'King Edward, by the grace of God, King of England, etc., and overlord of the Kingdom of Scotland, to his faithful and beloved Peter Burdett, keeper of the Castle of Berwick, salute. We order you, that you cause to be delivered without delay to the aforesaid John de Baliol, or his attorney, bearing these letters, the seisin of the aforesaid Castle of Berwick with all its purtenances, along with all other things delivered to you by chirograph, according as you have, received the things belonging the same in the aforesaid committed to your care.'

On the same day on which Edward issued this order in the Great Hall of the Castle, he broke the old Seal of Scotland into four parts, and putting them into a leather bag, had it placed in the treasury of England, to be preserved as a monument of his sovereignty over Scotland.

Berwick

Balliol swore fealty to him the next day at Norham and, after he was enthroned King at Scone Palace, later that month on St Andrew's Day, November 30th, he was obliged once more to swear fealty to Edward at Newcastle, with Edward, nevertheless, still claiming overlordship of the whole country.

Edward I had hoped to dominate Balliol as a "puppet king", with Scotland a land subject to English rule as, the price of his arbitration, demanded that Scotland must become a vassal of England,(ie a feudal subordinate tenant to whom he has vowed homage and fealty). Edward was now taking an active role in Scotland's governance: taxation, feudal disputes, and even an invasion of Flanders was mooted. Balliol, however, was successful in maintaining Scottish independence until 1294 when Edward demanded that he and other Scottish lords serve in his army against the

French. They refused, and Balliol would be formally removed from power.

    1295,the year that exacerbated the whole Scotland/England aggravation, began when Berwick's town mayor appended his and, subsequently, Berwick's signature to that of his King, John Balliol, in a new Scottish treaty with England's oldest enemy, France. King John of Scotland, John Balliol , whom King Edward1 had put on the Scottish throne in 1292 was by then regularly humiliated by him. In his desperation, at having various of his country's major settlements and fortifications confiscated by the English, John, in 1295, allied Scotland with the French against Edward, an act regarded, with some justification, as treachery by the latter. Edward I now regarded Scotland as rebellious and leaderless and, after the Scots had signed the first treaty of this diplomatic campaign, this 'auld alliance', with France in October 1295, he would invade Scotland to press his claims to his overlordship, which ultimately led to the horrific events of 1296, a date which should be etched on every Scot's conscience as much as Bannockburn, Culloden or Flodden!

Berwick

Although the Paris Treaty, in 1295, had reignited the hostility between Scotland and England, the threat of war had been seeded long ago, amidst a dynastic crisis in the Scottish monarchy. The Scots and the English had, until then, enjoyed a relative peace, but cruel fortune had now put the Scots at the mercy of a fearsome English king. In England, they'd acquired a powerful new enemy.

Ushering in a bloody era, the Battle of Berwick in 1296 was the first battle in the First War of Scottish Independence, and a devastating defeat for the Scots. The consequences of Scotland's alliance with France would be realised as war would be Scotland's come-uppance for having sided with the French. War was to break out between the two kingdoms and Berwick was the first to suffer.

Berwick

The Massacre of Berwick, March 30th, 1296

In 1296, the town was part of Scotland, and an extremely important settlement too: huge amounts of trade, particularly with Scandinavia and Northern Europe, coming through the port of Berwick. That trade made the place prosperous, far more significant at the time than even Edinburgh. Economically, Berwick was the most important town in Scotland and it would soon also be the bloodiest. Here King Edward would massacre most of the inhabitants of Scotland's main trading post, making his point most forcibly. The Massacre of Berwick would force any survivors of the region to finally submit to his English rule.

There was a vision seen, a form of premonition, at Berwick, before Christmas, by some school-children, who were engrossed in their books. They saw Christ, beyond the castle, on the semblance of a cross all covered with blood from blows, and his face turned towards the habitations of the town.'

After a raid on Carlisle, the English, under Edward 1 of England, started the conquest into Scotland. Often called the sacking of Berwick, it would occur after a siege, on Good Friday.

King John Balliol, who had ascended to the throne, was a weak king, but he was nevertheless a king, something Scotland hadn't had since 1286. Edward I (Longshanks) had already conquered Wales, and he looked to Scotland as his next conquest. In 1296, amassing a fearsome army, he marched north with 30,000 infantry and 5000 cavalry, intent on defeating the troublesome Scots. King Edward I of England, the "Hammer of the Scots" then invaded Scotland with his invasion force , entering the town by surprise, where he spent the next three days ruthlessly killing almost the entire civilian population.

Berwick

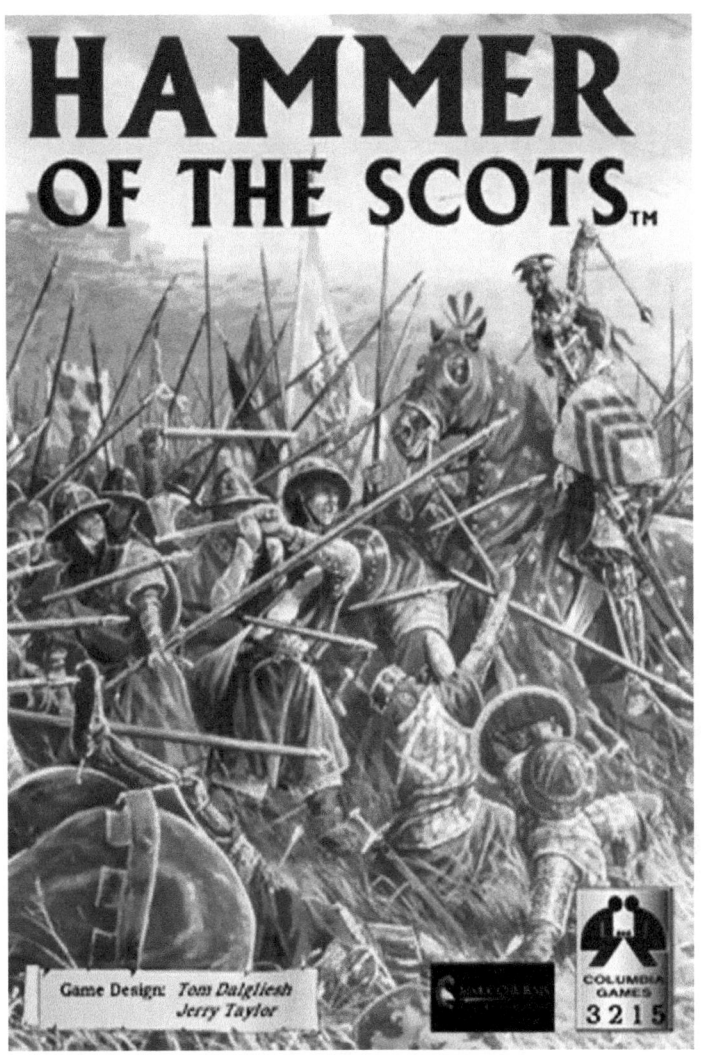

Kevin Scott

Berwick

Edward I. at Berwick.

At first, the ramparts had been crowded with armed citizens, when the large English fleet had been seen bearing round Lindisfarne. Only a few hours later, the hostile vessels would then enter the river's estuary, whereupon they then commenced a furious attack upon the town. Their assault was returned, initially, by the inhabitants as men who were resolved to die for liberty. The attacks of the English army were desperate, but without success, for desperate also were the men who opposed them. Thus, though they were being attacked upon both sides, the besieged garrison fought with the courage of surrounded lions, and the proud fleet was defeated and driven from the river. For hours the battle raged, and the Tweed became a sheet of blood. Several of the English ships were burned, while the rest, gliding back with the receding tide, escaped.

But, while the conflict rose fiercest, again the Bell Tower sent forth its sounds of death. Edward, now warned of the burning of his ships, and further roused by the taunts of the citizens, had proceeded with Berwick's immediate assault. Edward, at the head of thirty-five thousand chosen troops had, previously, crossed the river at Coldstream, and was now to be seen encamping at the foot of Halidon Hill. Part of his army, attacking from the north, commenced the descent upon the town, to the assistance of his fleet, while the greater part of the Berwick garrison held bloody combat with the ships in the river.

Berwick

King Edward, having now surrounded the town, demanded that the inhabitants surrender, but they would have none of it and showed their defiance by lining the walls and turning their backs on the great English king. It is recorded that they dropped their nether garments and presented their rear ends to the formidable warrior, a monarch who was feared throughout Europe. At this insolent gesture Edward, without further ado, encouraged his army to take the initiative by putting spurs to horse. There seems to have been little resistance. The King, as "rabid as a boar infested with the hounds", issued the order to spare none; and stories tell how the citizens would fall like the leaves in autumn, until there was not one of the Scots left who escaped alive, with King Edward rejoicing over their fate, as a " just judgment for their wickedness."

The defences of the town were merely a stockade and a ditch, so low and narrow that Edward, himself, had leapt over both and entered the town at the head of his forces. Though first over the walls, it must be said that, in 1296, there were many places in the Berwick Walls that were easy to breach. His following army then slaughtered, at will, the poor town's inhabitants. Edward had ordered his men to kill 7,500 souls of both sexes, and to make the mills "flow with the flow of their blood."

Berwick

(Medieval manuscript illustrating the siege and capture of Berwick in 1296)

The castle's garrison, commanded by William Douglas "the Hardy", could do nothing in their defence, their resistance futile, his men not standing a chance, whilst the English were under Robert de Clifford. Treachery however, that, to this day, remains undiscovered, existed in the town and, at an hour when the garrison thought not, the gates were deceitfully opened, and the English army rushed like a torrent upon the streets. Edward would storm Berwick Castle and its town "walls" (actually a wooden palisade) relatively easily, Edward's men making light work of the town's walls. Earth and wood soon came down as the town was massacred. It was a merciless sacking; men, women and children were slaughtered in the sort of acts that would earn Edward the nickname of 'Hammer of the Scots.'

Wildly the work of slaughter continued, with much bloodshed. With the sword and with the knife, the inhabitants defended every house, every foot of ground. The war of blood raged from street to street, while the English army poured on like a ceaseless stream. Shouts, groans, the clang of swords, and the shrieks of women mingled together. Fiercer grew the close and the deadly warfare, but the numbers of the besieged became few. Heaps of dead men now lay at every door, each with his sword glued to his hands by the blood of an enemy. The streets ran deep with blood; and independent of slaughtered enemies, the mangled and lifeless bodies of seventeen thousand of the inhabitants, men women and children paved the streets. The war of death would cease only from a lack of lives to prey upon. Edward's army would slaughter almost everyone who resided in the town, even if they fled to the churches, some eight thousand inhabitants being put to the sword there alone. The inhabitants of Berwick were butchered en masse. Some accounts state that as many as 17,000 men, women and children lost their lives and that "the city ran with blood like a

Berwick

river". Contemporary reports of the death toll vary hugely: depending on the source they run from roughly 7,000 to 60,000, though given the population of Berwick at that point, though most people say the population was up around 20,000 at this time.

Tales of the brutality abound: women and children being put to the sword; thousands being hanged; buildings burned with those inside perishing in the flames. The bloodshed lasted three days while every hiding place was searched and all those found were slaughtered. The churches afforded no shelter to those who fled into them. After being defiled by the blood of the slain, and spoiled of all their ornaments, it was most notorious that the King and his followers made stables of them for his horses, as well as lodgings for his army. Edward had been merciless and brutal in the destruction of the town and its inhabitants, butchering and putting to the sword anyone and everyone in the worst massacre by a state in the history of the island of Britain. More than even the Romans, Saxons, and Vikings had ever done. The last men to hold out were a body of Fleming merchants, who had done much to develop the trade of the town. They held out in the "Red Hall of Commerce"(now Woolmarket),but to no avail as they would all also perish in their Hall, when it too was destroyed by fire. Thus fell the Red Hall, and with it the commercial glory of Berwick. "From that time", states Eddington a local chronicler, "the greatest merchant city in Scotland sank into a small seaport."

Berwick

T oday, the fragmented medieval ruin of Berwick Castle stands, forlornly, beside the Victorian train station and Royal Border Bridge, now only a shell of its former glory, originally once that great Scottish fortress fought over by the Scots and the English for centuries. If it's stones could talk, what tales they could tell; invasions, massacres, wars, hostage taking and the like. When the castle had finally fallen, and Douglas had surrendered, surprisingly, Edward let the Scots garrison flee with their lives spared, Sir William Douglas was then imprisoned or incarcerated in the "Hog's Tower", and the town was given up to plunder and brutality. Berwick was ruined, the town would never regain its previous prosperity. Corpses were dumped in huge numbers in the sea and, now, the greatest merchant city of Northern Britain would sink, from this time, into a petty seaport.

It would, in time, be re-peopled with English traders and the remnants of the Scots who swore allegiance to the King. Edward remained in it for about three weeks after its capture. His first object was to put it, along with the whole district, into a thorough state of defence. On April 2nd, two days after the capture, he appointed Robert de Clifford, Warden of the March of Scotland, with a force of 140 horse and 500 footmen. He then determined, for the defence of the town, to dig a deep and wide foss around it, from the Tapee Loch (where the engine-sheds, etc., of the North British Railway now are), by the back of the town, to its exit on the pier road at the present Malt House. The foss was made eighty feet broad and forty feet deep. For this purpose the King summoned labourers from the county of Northumberland. The date of the writ (4th April) showed Edward's quick determination to do work when once he saw its necessity. The writ was addressed to the Sheriff, and commanded him to procure foss-workers, masons, carpenters, and all manner of artificers for his work at the foss with the workmen to occupy the places in the town of those slain in the massacre.

He issued another order from Berwick before he proceeded to chastise the whole kingdom of Scotland. On the ninth of the same month, he commanded all vagrants and criminals to join his army against Scotland, on the ground of a free pardon for such crimes as homicide, robberies, and transgressions of the forest laws!

The English, having captured Berwick, would then begin marching on Dunbar, where they would defeat another Scots army, before setting about their capturing of other Scottish castles, marching up as far as Elgin, before removing the most important symbols of Scotland's national identity - its royal regalia, crown jewels, documents and the Stone of Destiny. On the 10th July 1296, Edward forced

Balliol to surrender Scotland and the homage of all its people. This was to be enforced by oaths of allegiance to Edward himself. The alleged "Stone of Destiny", used to crown the Scottish kings, had also been stolen from Scone Palace by the English and since taken to London. The Earl of Douglas, under duress, swore allegiance to King Edward to escape imprisonment, but later in 1297 would join William Wallace in his rebellion against the English invaders.

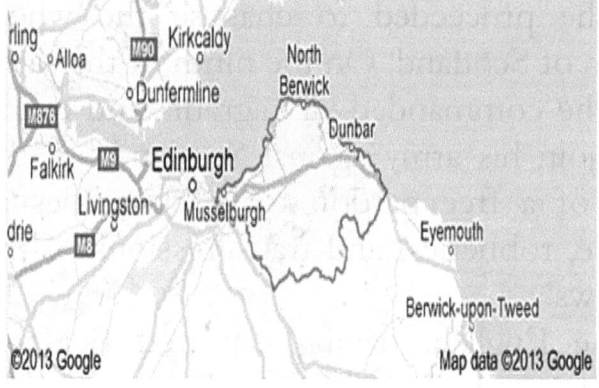

Berwick

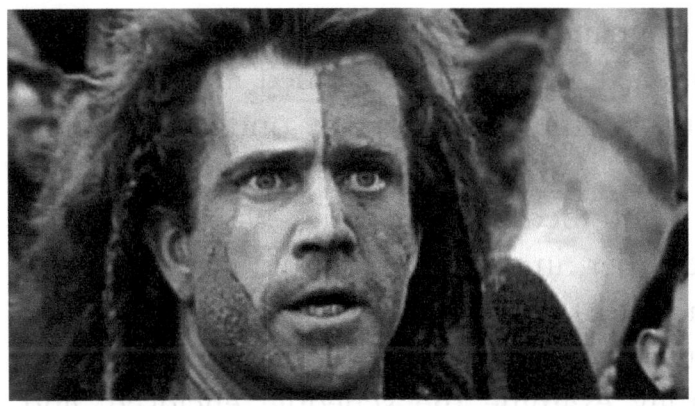

King Edward, having reduced Scotland to subjection, returned to Berwick and summoned a Parliament to assemble there on 23rd August, 1296 to settle the government of the Kingdom he had overrun and to receive formal homage from some 2,000 Scottish nobles, after defeating the Scots at the Battle of Dunbar in April and forcing John I of Scotland (John Balliol) to abdicate at Kincardine Castle the following July. The "homage" was not received well, and the "Ragman Roll" as it was known, earned itself a name of notoriety in the post-independence period of Scotland.

He also, there, made arrangements in a Parliament, for the carrying on of the government of submissive Scotland. Warenne, Earl of Surrey, he appointed Guardian of the realm, Walter de Agmondesham, Chancellor, Hugh

Cressingham, Treasurer, and Ormesby, Justiciar; and, at Berwick, he formed an Exchequer exactly on the model of the one at Westminster:

"And because the King wishes that the same order, in all things, should obtain as well in the said Exchequer in Berwick, as in that at Westminster, he orders that the barons should carefully examine the schedule enclosed, and those things, necessary for its establishment, will be sent as soon as possible, in order that they may have, in those things, the same order in the said Exchequer at Berwick, as is observed in the aforesaid Exchequer at Westminster."

As long as Berwick was a separate and independent town, a kind of conquest of England, yet lying in Scotland beyond the boundaries of its southern kingdom, it pleased the English King and his counsellors to keep in Berwick this Exchequer and its treasurer, and the other officers mentioned, as if it were a little kingdom of itself.

Warenne, the guardian, wrote that those "on this side of the Scottish sea" are coming to Berwick to complete the Covenants concerning the above peace; and he again alluded to Sir William Douglas, who was in good irons and

Berwick

safe keeping in the Castle of Berwick, because he did not produce his hostages when the others did. This Douglas was the same who had commanded the Castle of Berwick when Edward had taken it in the previous year. He was liberated on parole at that time, before next being found in the company of William Wallace, and was taken by Percy in Ayrshire, along with a number of Scottish nobles. Percy and Clifford brought him to Berwick, where they came in the summer of that year; and this last letter of Warenne's was written just as he set out from Berwick on his Scottish expedition beyond the sea. In the expedition he had a large host, among whom was found Cressingham. The latter gloried in pursuing the Scots and harassing them in every possible way. Warenne later would meet Wallace at Stirling Bridge, 1297, fighting out that battle with a fatal result to the English and to Cressingham, who was there killed and barbarously used by the revenging Scots.

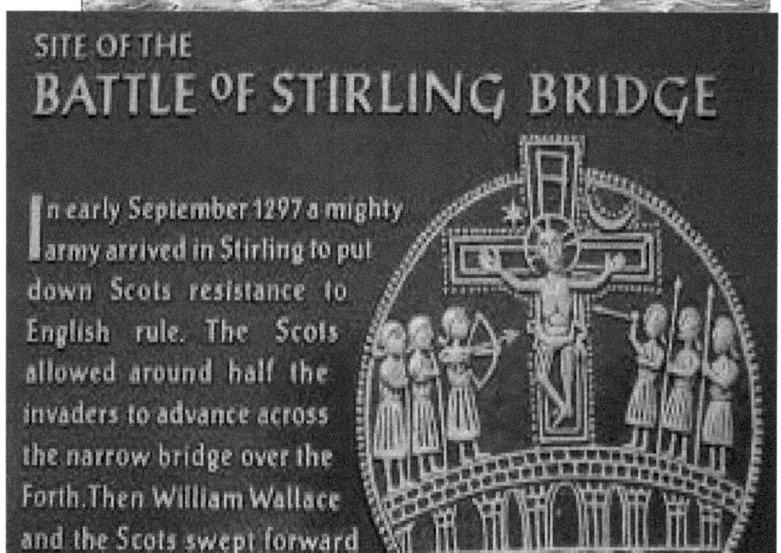

SITE OF THE BATTLE OF STIRLING BRIDGE

In early September 1297 a mighty army arrived in Stirling to put down Scots resistance to English rule. The Scots allowed around half the invaders to advance across the narrow bridge over the Forth. Then William Wallace and the Scots swept forward

Warenne rode off from that field of battle, and never halted till he reached Berwick. He had ridden so fast, so utterly had his courage failed him, that, when he stabled his horse,

Berwick

it immediately fell from exhaustion and expired. Warenne, soon after this, set out for England, and left Berwick undefended. The English inhabitants fled out of it; a Scottish force came into possession without any trouble, under a person named Haliburton, who kept it until Wallace himself returned from wasting Hexham in the early winter of 1298. The town remained quietly in the hands of the Scots all winter; but the approach of spring threatened likewise to bring an English force to recover the town; so the Scottish garrison fled. When the English came in the summer to its gates, they found it evacuated and ready to receive them. Only the town capitulated and recapitulated, for the castle had remained in Edward's hands all this time, well defended by its English garrison.

    This castle was not only well defended, but well provisioned, according to the King's orders. But the keeping of garrisons in Berwick cost the King much money, which he had increasing difficulty in paying. We learn that when Berwick came again into his hands, in 1298, he was then in debt, for his earls, barons, and soldiers, the sum of £28,966. Two gentlemen advanced the money; and the King gave them the customs of so many towns for payment, including those of Berwick.

I have said that the provisioning of the castle was abundant. It was more so for Berwick than for other places, for we find that large quantities of provisions were sent from it to other castles by the King's commands. On May 28, 1298, before the Battle of Falkirk, and just when the army was in Berwick awaiting Edward's arrival from Flanders, the keeping of the castle was given to Patrick, Earl of Dunbar, who had remained steadfast in his allegiance to the King.

1296-8, the English King , Edward 1, had Berwick Castle rebuilt and the town fortified, before it was returned to Scotland. The rubble of that, not that well, defended town was used to build English fortifications, the first town walls being built during his reign. Edward 1 was, without doubt, the premier monarch in the whole of Europe. Edward had ordered the massacre as an example to the rest of Scotland of what to expect should resistance to his overlordship continue. It was a coldly calculated act of inhumanity; the use of terror for political ends. He was renowned for his military prowess, seemingly second nature to the Plantagenet kings, and his command of the law. His mind followed a legal bent, a fact that would weigh heavy on the Scottish nation within the next few years.

It was a day that would be forever ingrained in Scottish memory. This was an end to the great city of merchant-princes; and Berwick was henceforth to hold the position of a common market town, and be conspicuous only, after the usual fate of a frontier town, for its share in the calamities of war. Yet, following the events of 1296, the Scots found a spirit which would not be subdued. Edward insisted that historical evidence proved he was their Overlord; that he was Lord Paramount over Scotland but eventually, following many a setback, the Scots would fight back. To some degree, some say, this had helped unite the Scots against the English. The sack of Berwick would eventually kick-start the Scots into a concerted defiance of the English king, whom they would come to view as an aggressive, warmongering imperialist. They refused to yield, they would not lie down. From these notions of resistance, unity and blossoming national pride sprang such men as William Wallace and Robert the Bruce to further cement the hearts and minds of the Scots against the

English. Edward I's conquest of Scotland now, very quickly, met with opposition, Wallace then becoming Guardian of Scotland, and viewing himself as Balliol's deputy.

Berwick

It was in the year 1295 that a young William Wallace had begun his armed struggle against the English menace. History books, and the film "Braveheart", have dealt with his lifestory but his connections with Berwick are what interest us here. In 1297 William Wallace (Braveheart) and Andrew Murray, had led the Scots to an historic victory over the English at Stirling Bridge on 11th September, before moving southwards to capture, briefly, the town of Berwick in 1297, but was unable to retake the castle, and was finally forced to retreat, abandoning the castle in the face of superior English forces.

Although also losing out the following year, 1298, at the Battle of Falkirk , the momentum was now firmly under way in Scotland's fight back against the hostile English occupation of her country. Wallace was replaced as Guardian by Robert Bruce, Earl of Carrick, and John Comyn of Badenoch. He then appealed to the Pope and the King of France for support. Bruce initially joined the English in 1302, perhaps prompted by Wallace's (and Balliol's) increasing success before the Scottish Parliament submitted to Edward I in March 1304. The defining moment in their struggle for freedom would be at the Battle of Bannockburn in 1314, a resounding victory for Robert the Bruce, King of Scotland, and ultimate humiliation for King Edward ll of England. In the words of the song that has become virtually an anthem, to the Scots, "Flower of Scotland" 'Proud Edward's army' was sent 'homewards to think again'.

History shows us that after 1304, when the English had captured Stirling Castle, Sir William Wallace would be betrayed and captured near Glasgow, and, following his public execution in London, on 23rd August 1305, his body would be hung ,drawn, quartered castrated, disembowelled and beheaded for his campaign of rebellion, with his head placed on a stake above London Bridge, while the remaining four quarters of his body parts of his body were sent north to Scotland for public display in the four corners of the kingdom as a warning to any would-be Scots rebels. Eventually his left arm was ordered to be nailed and hung above the gatehouse of Berwick's town walls , displayed on a pike as a reminder of Edward's justice and as a warning to others not to defy the English kings.

There is, today, a Saint Andrews, Wallace Green, Scottish Church of Scotland sitting proudly in the centre of Berwick, named in commemoration of this auspicious historical event in Berwick's often violent history.

By this date, Edward I had been describing Scotland as a land, rather than a realm, suggesting his future intention of placing it now under direct English rule. Edward was also reluctant to grant English-held lands to his Scottish supporters, which may have encouraged Robert the Bruce, once more, to change sides and claim the throne for himself. Bruce would be crowned at Scone Palace on 25 March, 1306, but military defeats quickly forced the collapse of his rule.

In 1306 the Countess of Buchan, for the crime of crowning King Robert the Bruce at Scone, was kept imprisoned in a cage in Berwick Castle ,above the town's walls where, for four years, she was exposed to public view before being released. At the same time as this, Robert the Bruce's sister, Mary, was similarly held in a cage above Roxburgh Castle, another Scottish monument currently occupied by the hostile English.

In 1307, Edward I died en route to invade the west of Scotland. His son, King Edward II, lacking the military prowess of his father, turned back to England, giving the Bruce and his "Good Sir James" Douglas time to gather support for their growing rebellion. In 1312, King Robert the Bruce attempted to claim the town of Berwick again, but is thwarted by the barking of a dog making known his arrival, strangely similarly as to how Rome had been saved by the cackling of geese!

King Robert then moved on to recapture Edinburgh, Perth and Roxburgh all in 1313. So too,in 1314 ,did James Douglas, the Bruce's right hand man, also made an abortive assault on Berwick Castle, but was more successful in taking Roxburgh Castle using the same tactics, attacking at night with specialized rope ladders. Also in that same year, 1314, the Bruce defeated Edward II's army at the Battle of Bannockburn, near Stirling, after Edward11 of England had mustered 25,000 men at Berwick who later both fought in and lost the battle. Scottish independence assured, and the English routed, Edward 11 also fled to back to Berwick, following this famous defeat at the hands of the Bruce. Edward 11 as he was pursued by Douglas, fleeing firstly to the coastal fortress of Dunbar where he and some of his men then escaped by boat to the security of Berwick, then still in English hands. By 1308, Bruce had regained the initiative, however, and began to expel the English from southern Scotland. His position as king was strengthened by his brilliant victory at Bannockburn on 24 June 1314, his armies now successfully capturing

Berwick in April 1318, with a truce with England being made in December 1319.

Berwick

However, on the 28th March 1318, Robert The Bruce was to prevail when, under the command of James Douglas, Berwick town was mastered and recaptured by the Scots , after the Castle was betrayed to the Scots by its incumbent English governor,(Sir Pierce Spalding delivered it up to Thomas Randall, Earl of Murray, April 2, 1318 in consideration of lands given him in Angus, in Scotland, starving its castle garrison into surrender ,in some small way, obtaining revenge for his father's death and the massacre of 1296.Here Bruce was to date many of his charters and assemble many of his parliaments, though the English were to make several unsuccessful attempts to recapture the Castle and Town the next year ,in 1319, when Edward11 laid siege in the July, but abandoned this by September.

Berwick is famous for its two sets of town walls. The first, of which only fragments remain, was built by Edward II, and was two and a half miles long; the second, which is the glory of Berwick, dates from the early years of Elizabeth, and is a mile and three-quarters in length. The ramparts completely surround the town, and there are only four gates_through the walls. The famous, medieval, Edwardian Walls were begun by Edward I; at least the ditch outside was dug by him; the wall was then built by Edward II, and strengthened by Bruce about 1320. It had nineteen towers and five gates and in Henry VIII's time was twenty-two feet high. The wall had an earthen embankment behind which was a retaining wall, forming the "Countermore". Entrance to the towers was through the Counter-more by a narrow passage supported by timber.

Berwick

Following on, we have the Declaration of Arbroath in 1320, which saw the Scots declare their determination to fight for their freedom in a letter to the Pope. The Treaty of Northampton of 1328 is traditionally viewed as bringing to a close, the Scottish Wars of Independence, it's now officially recognising Bruce's kingship and Scotland's independence of which the Battle of Bannockburn (1314) had been the decisive event. After his death, his son David became king, with the Earls of Moray and Mar as Regents. Conflict with England was, once more, renewed as Edward III now promoted a rival claimant to the throne, one Edward Balliol. The interval of peace would be short.

In 1329 Robert the Bruce, King of Scotland, died, leaving a minor (the future David11) as his heir. With the signing of the Treaty of Northampton in 1328, the First War of Scottish Independence had come to an end. As a result of the treaty, many nobles of associated with the Balliol and Comyn families lost their lands and titles in Scotland. In 1332, Edward Balliol, whose father, King John Balliol, had lost his crown following the Battle of Dunbar in 1296, raised an army in England and then invaded Scotland. Encountering Scottish forces, which supported young King David II, they won a decisive victory at the Battle of Dupplin Moor.

Berwick

Proclaiming himself King of Scotland, Edward Balliol found little support for his claim and was driven from the country after the Battle of Annan, that December. Returning to England, he appealed to King Edward III for assistance and promised to cede parts of south-eastern Scotland in return. Intrigued by the offer, Edward III renounced the Treaty of Edinburgh-Northampton and prepared to march north with the goal of supporting Balliol and reasserting English claims on Scotland.

Three years later, this rival claimant to the Scottish crown, Edward Balliol, with the secret backing of King Edward III of England, invaded Scotland and seized power. Balliol was however, within a few months, deposed in turn by a coup and fled to Carlisle. Edward III now prepared to give more overt support to his client, who in return affirmed an earlier promise to cede substantial tracts of Scottish territory to England. The chief concession by Balliol was the town of Berwick, which had been in Scottish hands since 1318. It was to secure this prize that , in May 1333, King Edward III arrived in person, to conduct the siege, the attack on Berwick now beginning in earnest. Seton carried out a spirited defence; but by the end of June, under repeated attack by land and sea, his troops were close to exhaustion. Scotland was now faced with exactly the same situation that

England had before Bannockburn ,and as a matter of national pride, Douglas would have to come to the relief of Berwick, just as Edward 11 had come to the relief of Stirling Castle in 1314.

The army, the "Guardian" had spent so much time gathering, was now compelled to take to the field, with all initiative lost. Nevertheless, Douglas' force was an impressive representation of the nation's strength and unity, with volunteers coming from all corners of the realm. As with all medieval armies the precise number of troops is difficult to estimate. It is possible, though, that the army was at least as strong as that which had fought at Bannockburn, perhaps even stronger. Douglas now began his belated march to the border. At the beginning of 1333 the atmosphere on the border was tense. England was openly preparing for war. In Scotland, Archibald Douglas, brother of the "Good" Sir James Douglas, and now Guardian of the Realm(regent) for the underage David, made arrangements for the defence of Berwick-upon -Tweed.

The Guardian's inactivity contrasts sharply with Robert Bruce's swift response to the siege of 1319. Alerted to English intentions, the Guardian of Scotland, Sir Archibald Douglas, who was ruling as regent for David, began raising the army and dispatched Sir Alexander Seton to defend the vital border town of Berwick-upon-Tweed. On March 10, 1333, Balliol crossed into Scotland at the head of an army and made for Berwick. Operating around the town, he was joined by Edward III in May after the English king had placed his queen at Bamburgh Castle for safety. Closing in on Berwick, the English entrenched and severed all of the town's supply lines.

While Seton's men fought off repeated English assaults, Douglas waited for the army to assemble before taking any action. With his defences near collapse, Seton agreed to a short truce with the promise that he would surrender on July 11 unless relieved. Douglas seems to have spent the time gathering a national army, rather than using the troops he already had in diversionary raids.

Weapons and supplies were gathered, and the defence of the town was entrusted to Sir Alexander Seton. The army quickly advanced towards Berwick, which was, immediately, placed under siege. Trenches had been dug, the water supply cut and all commu-

Berwick

nication with the hinterland ended. Balliol was now acting, quite openly, in the English interest.

The Scots attempted to draw Edward away from Berwick by Douglas conducting raids deep into England, at Bamburgh on July 11th, but Edward was not to be deflected from his aim. Douglas then destroyed the little port of Tweedmouth, which was then destroyed in full view of the English army. Edward did not move.

Edward III at the siege of Berwick

A small party of Scots led by Sir William Keith managed, with some difficulty, to make their way across the ruins of the old bridge to the northern bank of the Tweed. Keith and some of his men were able to force their way through to the town of Berwick. Douglas chose to consider this as a technical relief and sent messages to Edward calling on him to depart. This was accompanied with the threat that if he failed to do so the Scots army would continue south and devastate England. Again Edward did not move, so Douglas marched south to Bamburgh,

Edward refused to consider Keith's entry into Berwick as a relief in terms of the agreement of 28 June. As the truce had now expired, and the town had not surrendered, he ordered the hostages to be hanged before the walls, beginning with Thomas Seton, the son of Sir Alexander Seton, the Governor of Berwick in full sight of the garrison. A further two were to be hanged on each subsequent day for as long as the garrison refused to capitulate. Edward's determination had the desired effect. To save the lives of those who remained, Seton concluded a fresh truce, promising to surrender if not relieved by Tuesday 20 July. Everything now hinged on a Scots victory in battle. News

Berwick

of this was carried to the Guardian at Bamburgh where, having lost all freedom of action, he returned north into the very teeth of the wolf. Edward and his army took up position on Halidon Hill, a small rise of some 600 ft. two miles to the north-west of Berwick, which gave an excellent view of the town and surrounding countryside. From this vantage point he was able to dominate all of the approaches to the beleaguered port. Any attempt by Douglas to by-pass the hill and march directly on Berwick would have been quickly overwhelmed. Crossing the Tweed to the west of the English position, the Guardian reached the town of Duns on 19th July. On the following day, he approached Halidon Hill from the north-west, ready to give battle on ground chosen by his enemy. It would prove a catastrophic decision.

Memorial at the site of the Battle of Halidon Hill

Eventually, the Scottish authorities in Berwick appealed for a truce and after some dispute, about what constituted a breaking of the siege, it was agreed that if, by 20 July, the Scottish had not done one of three things i.e. won a pitched battle, effected a crossing of a stipulated stretch of the River Tweed or inserted 200 men-at-arms into the town, Berwick would surrender.

In reality the only option open to Sir Archibald Douglas, who led the Scottish field army, was to fight a battle and hope that, even if the English remained undefeated, at least the 200 men might be able to force their way into Berwick. To this end, on the last day possible, 19 July 1333, he made his move. From Halidon Hill, the height to the north which dominates Berwick, the English commanded the approaches to the town. Only by occupying the even higher ridge now known as Witches' Knowe, a mile further to the north, could Douglas have hoped to secure equally advantageous ground. Unfortunately, under the terms of the convention governing the relief of Berwick, the onus was on him to attack, so he could not remain on the defensive. This fact was to dictate both the form the Battle of Halidon Hill took and its outcome .The Scots suffered severe defeat despite being superior in number, Sir Archibald Douglas had approximately 13,000 men whilst King Edward led his army of 9000.

The Book of Pluscarden, a Scots chronicle, describes the scene:

They (the Scots) marched towards the town with great display, in order of battle, and recklessly, stupidly and, inadvisedly, chose a battle ground at Halidon Hill, where there was a marshy hollow between the two armies, and where a great downward slope, with some precipices, and then again a rise lay in front of the Scots, before they could reach the field where the English were posted.

The left was commanded by Balliol; the centre by Edward. Standing on the flanks of each division were six supporting wings of archers. Douglas' army was also arranged in three divisions, drawn up in traditional schiltron formation: the Guardian commanded the left; Robert Stewart, the future king, commanded the centre; and John Randolph, 3rd Earl of Moray the right. As Pluscarden says, to engage the English they had to advance downhill, cross a large area of marshy ground, and then climb up the northern slope of Halidon Hill. Although the Scots spearmen had proved their worth against cavalry at Stirling Bridge and Bannockburn, the battles of Dupplin Moor and Falkirk had shown how vulnerable they were to arrows. Not only was the ground bad, but it must have been obvious to the Guardian as he looked towards the massed ranks of Edward's archers that this was not going to be a cavalry battle. The prudent course of action would have been to withdraw and wait for a better opportunity to fight, but this would mean the automatic loss of Berwick. The Scots were now to fight one of the most disadvantageous battles in their history.

Berwick

No sooner had the Scots entered the marsh, at the foot of the hill, than the first arrows began to descend. They continued to fall intensely, in great clouds, as the Scottish schiltrons freed themselves from the marshy ground and began their ascent up Halidon Hill. Casualties were heavy, with some of the finest troops falling dead or wounded on the lower reaches of the hill. The survivors crawled upwards, through the arrows and on to the waiting spears.

It was Moray's depleted schiltron that first made contact with the enemy, closing on Balliol's division on the left. The Stewart followed, advancing on King Edward in the centre. Douglas came in their wake. As Douglas' men advanced down the slope and reached the marsh, the first English arrows began to descend on their ranks. Packed in tight lines and moving slowly, the Scottish troops suffered heavily as the archers continued to fire. Suffering heavy casualties, the survivors struggled up the hill toward the English. But even before Stewart and Douglas arrived, Moray's front ranks were failing in the hand-to-hand fighting with Balliol. The first to reach Edward III's men were from Moray's division. Badly depleted from the approach, Moray's men clashed with troops led by Balliol. Falling by the sword and continuing to take losses from the archers, Moray's men broke and began fleeing down the hill.

The panic from Moray's division soon swept across the Scottish lines as the arrows continued to fall. Soon Douglas' entire force was in full retreat. Rallying his highlanders, the Earl of Ross fought a gallant rear-guard action but was killed. With Ross' men overrun, the English knights mounted their horses and rode in pursuit of the fleeing enemy. While Stewart and Moray were able to escape, Douglas and five earls were killed in the fighting. With no let-up in the arrows, the schiltron broke, retreating rapidly downhill. Panic spread from the centre to the left. With English arrows directed towards the flanks the Scots bunched in a disorganised mass towards the centre, much as they had done at Dupplin Moor, as if each man was trying to hide from death behind the body of his comrade. Those in the rear began running back towards the marsh, away from the killing ground. Scots honour was saved by the Earl of Ross and his Highlanders, who fought to the death in a gallant rear-guard action.

With Ross gone, the English knights took to horse, riding off in pursuit of the fugitives. Stewart together with the earls of Moray and Strathern all managed to escape, but few others were as lucky. The battlefield was a grim place; the Guardian, Sir James's brother, Sir Archibald, lay dead with five other earls. They died in the company of the nameless commoners of Scotland, who fell in their thousands.

Scottish losses at the Battle of Halidon Hill are not known with any certainty, but they were extremely high and the army was effectively shattered. English casualties were light and have been reported as low as 14. The defeat at Halidon Hill stunned Scotland and the nation was essentially laid prostrate before Edward III as many of its leaders had been killed.

While many Scottish landowners were quick to swear fealty to the English king, Edward III did little to follow up his victory. As a result, the Scots were able to slowly recover and by 1335 scored victories at Boroughmuir and Culblean.

Berwick surrendered to Edward III one day later, while his protege, Edward Balliol, was reinstated as the King of Scotland. David II of Scotland now went into exile in France. News of Halidon Hill's defeat sent shock waves across southern Scotland, Edward soon to receive the fealty of several important landowners in the area. In England the victory, the first for many years, brought a great boost to the morale of the nation. Bannockburn had finally been avenged.

Edward's victory at Halidon Hill was a more devastating blow to Scotland than his grandfather's had been at Dunbar. After Dunbar most of the nobles had been captured and lived to fight another day; after Halidon most of the country's natural leaders were dead, and the few who remained were in hiding. Scotland was prostrate. It was said at the time that the English victory had been so complete that it marked the final end of the Northern war, for

Edward did little to exploit his success, but Scottish resistance, though weak, would never be fully extinguished. In 1342, we see records of Edward III spending his Easter at Berwick and hosting a jousting match with his Scottish knights.

The Scots, however, would not, ultimately, invade northern England until October 1346 when, on 7th October, the Scots entered England with approximately 12,000 men. They were expecting to find northern England relatively undefended because Edward III was, by then, conducting a major campaign in France. So after bypassing Carlisle, there being paid protection money, the Scots moved on further towards their ultimate goals of Durham and Yorkshire. After more than a week's march, they had sacked the priory of Hexham, before they were to arrive, to the west of Durham, on 16th October, ready for battle the following day. This meeting would be called the Battle of Neville's Cross.

Once again the Scots' poor strategic position on the battlefield would be their undoing , resulting in their formations falling apart as soon as they had advanced, allowing the English to deal easily with the Scottish attack. When it became clear that the battle was going in favour of the English, Robert Stewart and the Earl of March fled, abandoning David II's battalion to face the enemy alone. Later in the afternoon, the King's own battalion attempted to retreat, but was unsuccessful and David II was captured, while the rest of the Scottish army was pursued for more than twenty miles.

The Chronicle of Lanercost recorded that "few English were killed, several Scottish nobles were killed, including: 1,000 Scots were killed in the battle." David II had initially managed to escape, but was then captured by a John Copeland, the leader of the detachment out searching for him. Later, King Edward III ordered Copeland to bring the prisoner Scots king to Calais and hand him over, whereupon he then rewarded him with a knighthood and a handsome annuity. King David II was brought back to England and imprisoned at Odiham Castle in Hampshire from 1346 to 1357. After eleven years, in October 1357, a treaty was signed at Berwick by which the Scottish estates undertook to pay 100,000 marks (approximately £15 million in 2006), as a ransom for King David's release. David also agreed to name Edward III, of England, as his successor, which was rejected by the Scottish people, as evidenced by the continuing cross-border raids. After the death of Robert I, the conflict between England and Scotland would continue in a pattern of raiding, occasional invasion, battles and 'cold war'. The Treaty of Berwick of 1357, however, guaranteed a ten-year truce between the two countries, which began a period of uneasy peace that lasted, with frequent interruptions, until 1482.

In 1355, Sir Archibald's son, William (later 1st Earl of Douglas), with Patrick Dunbar, Earl of March and William Ramsay of Dalhousie routed almost the entire English garrison from Norham, in an ambush at the Battle of Nisbet, near Duns. Fearing for the security of the token garrison left at Norham, the English unwittingly sent out most of their troops from Berwick. Instead, though, the Scots, led by Dunbar ,and much against William Douglas's wishes, stormed Berwick town, briefly retaking it, before setting it ablaze as they were unable to secure the castle and finally had to withdraw, abandoning it when, more threateningly, English reinforcements (under Edward III) suddenly arrived. In February, 1356, Edward III retook Berwick and torched the Lothian countryside in reply, many Scots villages being burnt in reprisal attacks. It was around this time, in 1368, that Berwick also ceased to be a royal borough of Scotland. King Robert (Stewart)II now assumed the throne on David11s death in 1371.

November 30th 1378, and there was to be a more daring and successful assault made upon Berwick Castle, the raids becoming, every year, more destructive, whilst both sides, allegedly, desired peace. Percy and Sir John Gordon met at Berwick this year to arrange the terms of an armistice ,as the basis of a more enduring peace, when the news suddenly burst upon them that fifty Scottish desperadoes had suddenly surprised Berwick Castle, which caused all thoughts of peace to be laid aside. These Scots were to only hold it for eight days after Squire Alexander Ramsay of Dalhousie, had seized Berwick Castle by scaling the walls at night and surprised the bewildered garrison , who abandoned their posts and fled to Berwick Town. Robbers of the Scottish March thus entered, furtively, the Castle of Berwick, through a certain "foramen" of a certain tower, and finding the Constable of said Castle, Sir Robert de Boynton, a stout soldier, then unprepared, slew him, but permitting his wife and family to escape, upon condition of paying 2,000 marks within the three following weeks, or otherwise render their bodies in prison.

After the battle, William Douglas knighted his son James, since he had proved himself in battle. Archibald also knighted some of the other squires in the euphoria of victory and the prospect of much gold and silver for Musgrave and the other hostages safe return. The English complained "the Earl of March and Douglas and the latter's cousin, Sir Archibald, are harassing the English Borderers by imprisonments, ransoms and otherwise".

The Earl of Northumberland having heard of these proceedings hastened to besiege these malefactors, and without delay made an assault against the Castle placing himself, and his eldest son Henry (later the infamous "Hotspur" Percy), at the great gate of the Castle ,where they proceeded to fight those within, with stone-throwing and other warlike machines for a long time.

Ramsay had then found himself in a bit of a dilemma ,as the town was still held by Governor Thomas De Musgrave, who then called on the Earl of Northumberland and his army, said to number in their thousands, being drawn from as far away as Alnwick and Warkworth, to besiege the castle. Ramsay and his men made a stout resistance but lacking sufficient manpower and munitions it was only a matter of time until they were defeated. Neither did the courage of the besieged fail them, for they repelled the English who were opposed to them bravely and manfully, and drove them from the breaches for more than two hours. At length, after a severe and long conflict, the traitors were miraculously captured , with the castle's walls breached, it being entered by storm and all the Scots slain aside from Ramsay who was taken hostage as a bargaining chip to be used in ransom deals yet to be made between the Scots and English Borderers. Of the English, two were slain and many wounded, but of the Scots "there were slain forty-eight, one only being reserved to life who betrayed the counsels of the Scots to our men". The Earl of Northumberland taxed the Earl of Dunbar with giving aid to the Scots, but Dunbar denied all complicity, and said he would assist the Earl to undo the Scots.'

The seizing of Berwick Castle appears to have been done without the permission of King Robert II of Scots (1371-1390) or the Border lords, whose responsibility it was to protect the peace, but also to wage war when the time and prize was right. An organised combined attack on Berwick by the Scots, should have involved taking the castle and town at the same time with enough men and supplies to hold both against the evicted English. Ramsay's actions, though daring, would cause more trouble than they were worth as the English would, by Border tradition, have to retaliate in an "eye for eye" policy. So the whole Scots border was on alert for the counter attack which could come anywhere and at any time. Ramsay was not popular, for this reason, on both sides of the border.

Despite this, his Uncle Archibald "the Grim" Douglas (an illegitimate son of the "Black" Douglas) and Lord Lyndsay of the Byres, massed a relief army at Haddington, little more than 500 in number and marched south to Berwick hoping to collect more men on the way. But many of the Scots borderers were hostile to a rescue attempt, or diversion to help Ramsay escape, as they felt that he deserved to be captured by the English for his rash act. When Archibald's army approached Berwick his scouts informed him that the English army encircled around the castle numbered around 10,000 strong with archers, siege engines, heavy horse and ships blockading the river, and that there was no avenue of escape for his nephew. Archibald then made a lengthy speech to his army, praising Ramsay and his men as heroes but that, in all fairness, it would be suicidal for them to engage the English in open battle or even attempt a diversion, as they were totally outnumbered. Reluctantly, the army withdrew heading towards Melrose, to support local forces there in resisting the expected English counter attack.

King Richard's protection still extended over the burgesses. He was kind and reasonable—at least his Council of Government was, with the Duke of Lancaster at its head. In 1383 the Council extended its benevolence to Berwick in a manner certainly worthy of note, not so much for the amount of the gift as for the reason given for it. A subsidy or new tax had been levied over the whole kingdom, of 2s. on every hogshead of wine and 6d. on every pound weight of merchandise. But the Council said, 'We wish you to be exonerated of this tax because, first, Berwick is situated beyond the limits of the kingdom; secondly, the men of this same town are not accustomed to come to our Parliament; and thirdly they add, of right you ought not to be burdened with this subsidy.' No representation, no taxation.

The history of Berwick, in 1384, seems dark and troubled, and difficult to unravel. It seems that the Scots had burned the town in the month of May or June, but had obtained no possession. This is shown by a letter written by James Douglas, Lord of Dalkeith, Warden of the Marches of Scotland. Richard complained to him of the infraction of the truce then existing between the two countries. Douglas wrote Richard a characteristic letter, defending his conduct and accusing Richard of allowing his men against all honesty to 'herry' Scotland. but regained by same rather quickly.

Later in the year, 1384 the Scots gained possession of Berwick Castle and Town, it is said, by bribery. Northumberland's Deputy-Governor, Earl Percy, suffered himself to be bribed to deliver up this stronghold to the King of England's enemies. The King, and especially Lancaster, who still nursed his wrath against the Earl, were angry at the loss and Berwick's betrayal to the Scots. The treacherous commander of Northumberland was summoned to appear at London to answer for his remissness of duty. He, unsurprisingly, preferred to remain in the north, saying that the Marches needed his presence, as he knew, on the other hand, that his going to London might involve the loss of his head. But, gathering from the tone of the King and Parliament that they were in earnest, the Earl immediately set himself to recover Berwick. The weather was too unpropitious to lay a regular siege, so he bribed the Scots with 2,000 marks to give up the Castle, which was done without delay. The charge against him,

Berwick

after this action, was dropped, resulting in the King, both pardoning and restoring him to his favour.

In the opening months of the next year,1385, with a relative quietness once more prevailing in Berwick, the King was anxious to repair the ravages made by the Scots soldiers when, in the early part of the past year, they had burned down the town. In January, Commissioners were appointed to report on the state of the fortifications, and to inspect the men-at-arms and archers in the garrison of Berwick. In March the inhabitants were asked to repair the damages out of their local taxes. We hear no more of Berwick's outward, and military, history till Richard is deposed, and Henry Bolingbroke assumed the reins of power as King Henry IV, King of England, in 1399.

During this interval, Berwick gained a breathing-time to set its house in order. In what state the streets were kept at this period, it is impossible to say. In later years the subject would become plain enough but, for now, all available information is fragmentary. In 1387 an order was issued by the King, conferring on the burgesses the right of levying taxes .In 1390, Robert 111 became the Scottish King whilst in England, King Henry was to continue all the Berwick officials, and confirm their appointments. The same regulations, as in King Richard's reign, served to guide the Custom House officers in levying the taxes on wool. The three divisions were still the same: (1) Between the Tweed and Coket; (2) The English districts in Scotland; (3) The purely Scottish districts.

King Henry IV had so much more difficult work on hand, that the constant intermeddling with Berwick's trade ceased. In ordinary circumstances, the trade in wool ought now to have largely increased, but the military display and activity that had grown rapidly, from century to century, was now proving a powerful counteracting influence to the natural development of trade. The Northumberland family had, for a lengthened period since 1333,

Berwick

held the Governorship of Berwick, and Wardenship of the East Marches. The Earl, in company with Neville, Earl of Westmoreland, had headed the conspiracy against King Richard II, and it was they who had set Henry IV on the throne.

For services rendered, Northumberland would now be suitably rewarded. Amongst other honours showered upon him, he was made Constable of England, Warden of the Western Marches, Sheriff of Northumberland, and also continued in his office as Warden of the East Marches, while his son, Harry Hotspur, was kept as Assistant-Governor of Berwick.

But, ambitious, haughty, overbearing, these nobles could brook no opposition and a cause of quarrel soon arose with the King. Hotspur, among the reasons of his discontent, asserted that he had not been fully satisfied of his wages as Governor of the Border town, nor had his father, as Warden of the Marches, He, in short, demanded £20,000 in redemption of the King's liabilities, a sum the King could not pay. The King knew himself to be a usurper on the throne, and dared not ask a subsidy, and he had no other means of gratifying Hotspur's intemperate demands. Stirred by undercurrents of hatred against the very King they themselves had elevated to the throne, the Percys again raised the standard of rebellion, and proceeded immediately to open warfare.

The said Henry Percy, with several of his accomplices, then came into the town of Berwick-on-Tweed, and by force took the keys of the same town from the Mayor and burgesses, and delivered or caused them to be delivered to the Scots—enemies of Our lord the King, and of his Kingdom of England— which Scots, by comfort; favour, and counsel of Henry de Percy and his accomplices, robbed

Berwick

and pillaged the said town and the inhabitants of it, and afterwards set fire to the same town.

Holinshed, the scribe, added that Berwick was sacked, and every house in it burned, save the Friaries and the churches. This was done by the Scots when Northumberland aided them in getting possession of it. That this burning of Berwick was severe, there remains little doubt, for, in December, 1405, 1,000 marks were given by the King's order to the burgesses from the customs of the town to make for emendation and reparation of the towncastle, houses and habitations alike, destroyed by the rebels and enemies.

They, likewise, then liberated Archibald, Earl of Douglas, who had been taken prisoner at the bloody field of Homildon, near Wooler, on condition that he would assist them in their rebellion, and in their attempt to put Mortimer upon the throne. Douglas was promised Berwick as a free gift in case of success. The battle-field of Shrewsbury, 1403, shortly afterwards saw the complete overthrow of the scheme, the death of Hotspur, the captivity of Douglas, and the enforced flight of the Earl of Northumberland, who had been prevented by sickness from fighting with his son on that fatal field.

The Castles of Berwick and Jedburgh were actually restored to his keeping in November of that year. But the spirit of revolt was unquenchable in the old man; he joined a new conspiracy to set the Earl of March upon the throne. His lands and possessions were once more confiscated, and he and his followers escaped north to Berwick. Thither, the King followed with large forces, and demanded the surrender of the Earl's castles as he proceeded. On coming to Alnwick, he summoned it to surrender; but the Captain called out, 'Wynne

Berwick

Berwick ones, and you shall have your entent'. The King passed on to Berwick, which Sir Wm. Graystock attempted to hold; but the first shot from a cannon of large bore demolished part of a tower, and caused such consternation that the garrison immediately surrendered.

The Earl, before this took place, had been asked by the King to deliver, or cause to be delivered to royal commissioners, the Castle of Berwick as well as the Percy Tower, the seal called

Coket, and the annual rent of 500 marks, payable to him out of the customs of Berwick. But instead of obeying the order, he left the castle in charge of Graystock, and set out for Scotland, taking with him the infant son of Hotspur. This child was cared for at the Court of Scotland. When the young Scottish King, not long after this, March 30th, 1405, was going to France for his education, young Percy was on board as his companion. Both were taken prisoners by Henry, and kept for a time as captives.

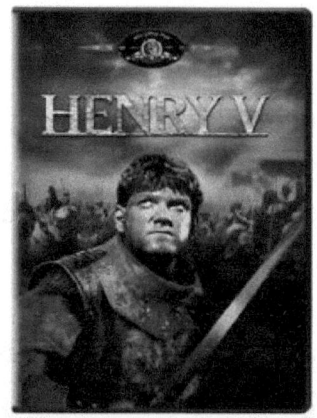

    This King's successor, the brave and energetic Henry V of England, took a liking to this young scion of a proud English earldom, and very soon restored him to his lands and honours. To return, the taking and re-taking of Berwick, at this time, seemed simple enough. Hiding for a time in Scotland, he was again drawn into active opposition, met the royal forces at Bramham Moor, and was there slain. Treated as a traitor, his body was quartered, and a portion of it suspended at Berwick, the scene of so much of his active life.

  The King, Henry V, had in short, as early as 1403, conferred the Wardenship of the Marches and the Governorship of Berwick upon his young son John, afterwards Duke of Bedford. He was only fourteen years of age when appointed, and in 1405, when he had served the office for two years, a grant of £1,000 was given him out of the tithes of York and Canterbury, for the safe keeping of Berwick and the East Marches. This liberal treatment did not last long, for we have from his pen, in 1409, a very strongly-worded letter to his father the King, urging payment of arrears and the propriety of putting the fortifications of the town into a proper state of repair. He says 'If any power or ordnance of the Scots or other shall be directed to assail the town and Castle of Berwick, they cannot be safely guarded, because they are neither repaired, stored, nor victualled, nor in any manner defensible, more particularly on account of the ruinous state of the walls and weakness of the gates and bridges. England's answer back to this financial funding plea, for the town's regeneration, by her governor was that "Berwick is in the realm but not of it".

A side note here is recorded in that Robert Boynton, who had been Constable of the Castle in 1378 ,and had lost both the castle and his head to a band of Scots, was followed by his son, Henry Boynton, who joined an insurrection against Henry IV in 1405 and also lost the war, his lands and his head.Robert and Henry, along with lots of co-conspirators, tried to escape the wrath of Henry IV by hiding in the castle . During the sacking of the town by the Scots in 1405 the whole town was burnt. Henry IV made a grant out of the town's customs for the Tollbooth to be repaired or rebuilt by the Burgesses.It is strange that this ruinous state of the town was allowed to continue, since their enemies, the Scots, were threatening them always so closely. The wars of the Borders not only harmed the town of Berwick, but the whole district.

In 1406, James1 became King of Scotland, however was captured by English pirates while at sea and, for 18 years, would be held captive in England, while his uncle, the Duke of Albany, would rule Scotland. James would not actually be crowned until 1424.

Berwick

1422 and King Henry V, of England, had died in France, and was succeeded by his son, a minor. The country was left to the government of a regency, when the Scots considered it a favourable time for once more assaulting Berwick. Murdoch, now the Regent of Scotland, approached Berwick and Roxburgh with considerable force, but made no impression on either of the towns or fortresses. The expedition ended much as the former had done, and was contemptuously called by the English the 'Dirtin Raid'. The Council of Regency in England was now favourable to the restoration of the Scottish King, and he was in March, 1423, accordingly delivered to the Scottish Commissioners at Durham, and is said to have come with a great train of English lords and ladies to Berwick, He was liberated for a ransom of £40,000 of good English money, which was to be paid in equal parts in the next six years. Out of the first payment that was made, the Earl of Northumberland, as Warden and Governor, received his salary, as well as the wages of the soldiers maintained by him for defence of Berwick and the East Marches.

The Berwick traders and merchants were now, by 1429, considering on how they were going to be entirely ruined by being forced to use Calais, by their English king, as their port of exchange and trade. The argument to support Calais as the staple for Berwick wools must be weak, when the writer had to appeal to the loyalty of the traders, and to the amount of royal blood, shed in its conquest. The argument was not strong, because the burgesses of Berwick got permission, shortly afterwards, to begin exporting whither they pleased, and to make the best bargain they could in any open port of Europe.

The English King now made a proposal to James of Scotland (1432) that, if

Berwick

adopted, would have changed the current of all the future history of the two nations but, like other proposals of a similar nature, it was rejected by the Scottish Parliament with scorn. Henry VI offered to deliver up the old Scottish counties of England —Northumberland, Westmoreland, and Cumberland—if the Scottish King would break with France, and join him in a league, offensive and defensive. On the refusal of this offer, it is said that the English ambassadors left Stirling without leave-taking, Berwick and the Borders then once again being made to suffer from the outbreak of the war spirit of the two nations.

The whole of this correspondence arose out of the raid of the Scots of the 3rd July, 1433, when they assembled in great force before Berwick, and then preyed upon the country, and took away with them '60 horses and 600 nowt.' The Kings continued for a year or two to discuss the question of reparation, when at length, in 1438, a truce was agreed upon, and acted on, as far as the keepers of the Marches on both sides were concerned. It came into force after a threatening of Berwick, by the King of Scots, in 1436, and an appointment of commissioners to observe his movements, and restrain them, if possible. This truce, ratified on 1st May, 1438, lasted seven years, and was continued afterwards for stated periods. In this truce, for the first time, some attempts were made to define the limits within which the soldiers and others, residing in Berwick, in the King's name, should have grass and hay for their beasts, as well as fuel and other necessaries. There is no doubt that, to this lack of proper definition, much of the quarrelling between Scottish and English may be attributed. There was now a boundary-line laid down—the same Bound Road that is now so well-known between the liberties of Berwick and Scotland.

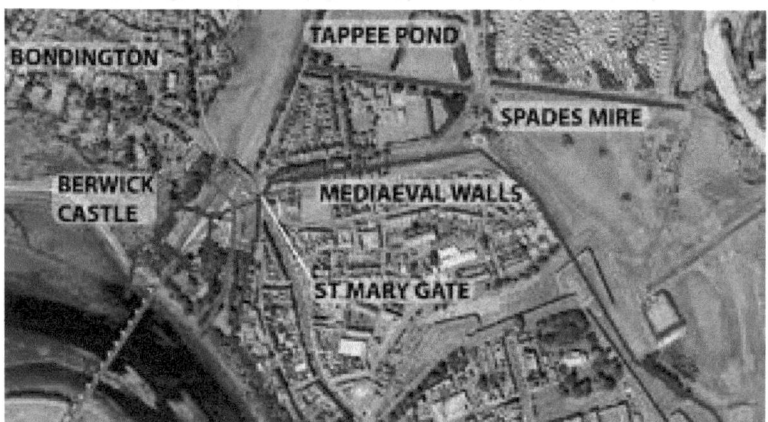

Berwick

In 1437 James11 became King of Scotland, following his father's murder, whilst in the following year, 1438, the Riding of the Bounds first takes place in Berwick an event which still occurs, annually, to this day. James was the first to make an advance to the Borders when, in the year 1455, he threatened Berwick, and must have advanced within easy reach of the town. James, with his host, had withdrawn upon show of opposition, to Roxburgh, where he actually entered upon the siege of that said castle.1460 would see James 11 being killed, while besieging Roxburgh, when a cannon exploded, James 111, then becoming king.

At this time, civil war was raging in England between the Yorkist and Lancaster factions, and King James II then made a secret treaty with King Henry VI, who was to give the northern king, Northumberland and Berwick in 1459, if he would assist him in his cause against his Yorkist enemies, in the Wars of the Roses. Consequently, we have raids into England by James which continued, until Henry was obliged to ask him to desist. When the Battle of Towton was fought on March 29th, 1461, at which the hopes of the Lancastrians were entirely crushed, the defeated King departed with

Berwick

his wife and son to Berwick, and leaving the Duke of Somerset there, continued into Scotland and asked for further aid from the Scottish King. The young King of Scots comforted him, and assigned him a competent place to live in during his abode there. Henry VI, in return for this kindness and friendship, delivered to the King of Scots the town of Berwick, as promised which would remain in his hands for next 21 years, during which we learn much concerning Berwick at that time.

Kevin Scott

When, in 1461, Berwick was recovered by the Scots, from Henry VI, one Robert Lauder of Edrington was put in charge of Berwick castle, an important official and soldier in Scotland at that time. The Haddington customs account, rendered in July, 1462, and going back to March, 1461, contains an entry that may perhaps be connected with the handing over of Berwick to the Scots—an item of £3 8s. 2d. as paid to the Keeper of the Privy Seal and other household servants of the King and Queen at Haddington, when they rode to Coldingham to confer with certain Englishmen, supposed to be commissioners empowered to deliver Berwick over to the Scots.

The same accountants credited themselves at the same time with various outlays expended on Berwick Castle at the time of its recovery, viz., the purchase and direct carriage of a quantity of salt, and the carriage of oatmeal, bombards and artillery, also destined for Berwick, to the Port of Belhaven, whence the goods were shipped to Berwick. In 1464 Robert Lauder was paid £20 for repairs made to Berwick Castle, whilst he, Lauder, would hold his position uninterruptedly for a full thirteen years at least, or until 1474, when he was succeeded by David, Earl of Crawford, one of the then most influential servants of the Scottish King.

    He retained his office for two or three years, and during his tenure he was given 300 marks, evidently to maintain the dignity of his higher rank. Again, in 1477, George Ker, of Samaliston, and George Hwme, of Wethirburn, were appointed Keepers of the Castle, after whom, on the 3rd February 1478 following, Robert Lauder, of the Bass and Edrington, keeper of the castle at Berwick-upon-Tweed with a retainer of £250 per annum . Lauder continued till the last year of Scottish occupation, when Patrick Hepburn, 1st Lord Hailes, had possession of the fortress.

    From the time that the Scots got possession of the town till 1476, the Keeper of the

Castle had held the office of Chief Customer. His wages were paid, as when the town was in English possession, out of the customs of the town, as far as these would answer the amount.

The English were, again, about to try and recover their old fortress. Edward IV of York was now King of England, and at his Court were two renegade Scots, Albany and Douglas, plotting against their own country, and urging on the English to recover Berwick. James, the Scottish King, had evidently given grounds for retaliation. He had made raids into the northern counties, and had forced the hand of his English neighbour. Afraid of losing Berwick, the Scottish Parliament eagerly seconded the King, in putting the town and castle into order. A tax of 1,000 marks was cordially granted to victual it. Warlike engines were made for defensive operations, the walls had been repaired, and a great portion newly built, so that when the English laid siege to it in 1481, the defence was so vigorously conducted by the Scots that the enemy was obliged to withdraw.

Next year, in 1482, affairs in Scotland became so complicated that there was no longer any possibility of withstanding the forces brought against the town. The King of Scot-

Berwick

land had been rendered powerless by the conspiracy completed at Lauder, when Archibald Douglas undertook to 'bell the cat' when James's favourites were mercilessly hanged over Lauder Bridge, when the army had dispersed which had gathered for Berwick's defence. During the reign of Edward the 4th, an English force of 22,500 men, commanded by Richard Duke of Gloucester, the future King Richard111 of England came against the town, to raid Scotland, after the Scots had burned Bamburgh in 1480. While the Earl of Northumberland led the van, other notable leaders, the Lords Neville, Stanley and Fitzhugh, along with the rebel Albany, took a share in this enterprise. 'The army marched forthwith and came suddenly by the waterside of the town of Berwick, and what with force and what with fear of so great an army, took and entered the town, but the Captain of the Castle would in no ways deliver it, holding off a 3 month siege.

The captains, then, decided to go on to Edinburgh with the main army, and left 4,000 to keep up the siege against the castle, it being finally conceded to England, after the 3 months, whereupon it was replaced under English administration. Richard then advanced to

Edinburgh where James 3rd of Scotland had been imprisoned, but did not have the siege capability to take it and so withdrew back to England, most probably, Berwick.

Lord Hailes, who had kept the castle in such a soldier-like fashion, evidently expected help from Scotland. In this he was greatly disappointed, and eventually withdrew, after surrendering the fortress to the English on August 25th, 1482. It is probable that he did this in the terms of the Treaty of Edinburgh, which not only included its surrender, but also stated that Albany should be reinstated and pardoned for his treasons. Thus Berwick passed, forever, from under Scottish rule into English possession and government. Although not officially merged into its kingdom, England has administered the town of Berwick ever since this date, though many today think its destiny should still lie north of the border, in Scotland.

Before the reign of Edward IV closed, he would confirm the charter of Edward III to Berwick, and all previous charters. Edward V nominally succeeded his father, but he was entirely ruled and controlled by the Duke of Gloucester, under whose directions the Earl of Northumberland was again appointed Warden of the East Marches and Keeper of Berwick town and castle.

The terms of his appointment gives us considerable information as to the garrison kept at that time. The Indenture bears date 20th May, 1483, and 'is maid betwix our said sovereign lord King Edward V and the right trusty and well-beloved cousyn, Henry erle of Northumberland: arraied, of whom 300 at least shall be archers. Five hundred of them shall be for defence of the town and one hundred for the castell. Two sufficient gentlemen arc to act as lieutenants, one for the town and one for the castell. The said erle for keping these safely shall have a reward, £438 10s. 11d.; £420 of this sum shall be for the pay of 600

When we proceed to the reign of Henry VII, the chief interest in or around Berwick was centred in the making of truces between England and Scotland in which, for the first time, Berwick had a clause all to itself, which clause has been seriously misunderstood. On its strength it has been, again and again, asserted that Berwick was now formed into an independent town, independent of both countries. But there is no such idea contained in the truces of that time. Here is the clause as it stands in the Treaty of London, the first of the series of truces confirmed in Henry's reign:

'Moreover it is agreed upon that, during the present truce for three years, or only one year, that the town and castell of Berwick shall stand and remain along with the inhabitants and dwellers of the same, in abstinence of wars and in truces of wars all the time of aforesaid truces, so that neither the most serene King of Scots for himself, nor any of his liege subjects or vassals, shall make war or attack or besiege the place. Nor shall the most serene King of England for himself, or any of his inhabitants of town or castell, in any way whatever make war, assault, or siege upon the said most serene King of Scotland, his lieges or vassals, in any way during the remaining time of these truces. The Party who does attack, or do any harm during these truces, shall be punished by the King to whom he belongs.'

This treaty was ratified in the Parish Church of Berwick. Next year, the same matter was again referred to in the treaties of marriage proposed to take place between (1) James, Earl of Ross, and Katerine, third daughter of the late King Edward IV, and (2) James III, King of Scotland, and one of the said King's daughters; so that by these marriages;

'By the grace of God to be completed sail folowe the final appeasing and cesing all sic debates betwix the Kings of the seid realmes for the time being movit and attempit. Of the quhilk castell and toun of Berwick, the said King of Scottis desiris alwaies deleverance at the final appeasing of the said marriages or any of them. These to be confirmed at Edinburgh, on the 24th of Jany, 1488 ; and then to be concluded, in the moneth of May, these marriage treaties, along with the appeasing of said matter of Berwick, as is aforesaid. The truces to be carefully kipt meanwhile, the said Town and Castell, with the limits of the same, to stand in sic special assurance trewis and abstinence of were as is comprisit in the indenture of the said trewis taken at London.'

King James, on his part, did agree, and would have carried out these treaties of marriage and truces, for he was very anxious indeed to repossess himself of the town of Berwick. Henry, on his part, drew back, and no such marriages ever took place. It shows the extreme anxiety of James to recover Berwick, when he actually agreed to marry a woman considerably older than himself; and it shows the high estimate that Henry VII put on Ber-

Berwick

wick, when all that hindered his fulfilment of the treaties was the demand of James that, before he would treaty, Berwick must be given up to his charge. Still, in all this, there was no word of rendering it independent of both countries, and these are the very words that occur in every treaty made about this time.

'But to counterbalance this the English possess beyond the eastern arm of the sea : named Tivide [Tweed], in the kingdom of Scotland, the singular fortress of Berwick, which, after having belonged for a considerable time to each kingdom alternately and at length had fallen into the hands of the Scottish, was made over to King Edward the Fourth by the Duke of Albany, who was at war with his brother, James III, King of Scotland. And now King Henry VII has built a magnificent bridge across the aforesaid arm of the sea, and as he has the command of all of the eastern coast he can throw as many troops as he pleases into the town, which is a very strong place both by nature and art. And as such Berwick has caused the death of many thousand men in former times.

The policy of Henry VII was directed towards reducing the power of the nobility, and this led to a decided change in the government of the town. Since 1333, when Berwick may be said to have come into English power, someone of the great English lords had been Warden of the Marches and Governor of the Town. But, in 1491, Henry appointed his eldest son Arthur, Prince of Wales, when a mere boy, to these important offices. In 1495 the same duties were conferred upon his second son Henry, Duke of York, who ultimately became Henry VIII of England. While these were in office, and even before this, deputy-governors were really the ruling powers in the town.

Berwick

We pass now to an interesting episode in our story. James IV. had been promised the daughter of Edward IV. for a wife ; but he was tempted by a richer dowry. Negotiations, long protracted, were now begun with the view of a marriage between the Scottish King James and Margaret, Tudor daughter of Henry VIII. The marriage treaty was drawn up, and eventually signed in 1501. Margaret was young, and this caused delay. In fact, she was only thirteen years of age when, in July 1502, she was sent into Scotland, where she was entertained in Berwick, whilst en route to her marriage to James the 4th of Scotland. The future queen was then taken to Berwick Castle, where she was received by Lady Darcy. The next two days were spent in Berwick, when the Captain treated her to good cheer and such amusements as the times afforded. Courses of chase within the town, bear-baiting and other gentlemanly sports passed the time away until she was delivered to the Scottish Commissioners at Lamberton Toll, on the Scottish border.

After spending two nights at Dalkeith, she was then taken to Edinburgh, near which the King met her, and took her on the pillion of his saddle, and so rode her through the streets of Edinburgh to Holyrood Palace, where they were married, after the fashion of kings,in 1503.

Berwick

Thereafter a Treaty of Perpetual Peace was signed between Scotland and England, with Berwick being given special status of "being of the Kingdom of England, but not within it," also needing special mention in later proclamations to this effect. This marriage is certainly very foreign to our story in one sense, but in another it pertains very closely to it. One hundred years after its celebration, it led to the elevation of James VI. to the throne of England, which eventually would unite the two countries and put a stop to the almost continual bloodshed that had prevailed for so long upon the Borders, and of which Berwick now became, more than ever, the very centre. The peace made at this time was to be perpetual. Berwick was now guarded in the marriage-treaty in the same manner as in the Treaty of London.

Kevin Scott

Other Notable Dates

1513. The Battle of Flodden, where an invading Scottish army was soundly beaten and King James IV of Scotland was killed, his slain body being brought back to Berwick, some 12 miles north-east.

1548. John Knox, founding father of the Protestant Reformation in Scotland, and of the Church of Scotland, appeared in Berwick as a preacher, where he stayed for 2 years.

1551. The town of Berwick was made a county corporate. King Edward IV and Queen Mary signed a treaty declaring that Berwick would continue to be ruled by England, but would still not become part of it!

1558 - 1570. The new defences were built around Berwick to protect the Protestant English, of Queen Elizabeth I, from the Catholic Scots and their French allies. Although the medieval walls had protected the town for over 250 years, these had enclosed a much bigger area, including the Castle, which once stood on the grounds of the present railway station.

The new Elizabethan Walls ended up cutting the town in half, with a gate the only way between. The ramparts were designed to mount the guns which defended the town during any conflict between the English and Scots. The Scots Gate was originally only one cart wide, with wooden doors and a drawbridge over a moat. A military checkpoint stood inside the gate, where the main guard of soldiers secured the town every night by closing the gate.

1560. The anti-French, Ty of Berwick was signed, in February, between England and Scottish Lords.

1566. Mary Queen of Scots in Berwick.

1586. The Ty of Berwick was signed, in July, which promised an annual grant to James VI of Scotland.

1592. The Mayor of Berwick complained that Scottish merchants were undercutting the English in the town and removing English coin into Scotland. The following year, all Scottish servants were barred from the town, and English soldiers with Scottish wives were dismissed. However, hundreds of Scottish people were still recorded as living in Berwick in 1597.

1603. When Queen Elizabeth1, of England, died, the English crown went to her next living relative, King James of Scotland . Berwick was the first English town to greet King James VI of Scotland on his way to being crowned King James I of England. Upon crossing Berwick Bridge, James is supposed to have again declared the town as neither belonging to England nor to Scotland, but part of the United Crown's domain, a fact of its non-return possibly surprising to many Scots as he passed through the town.

1611. The Old Bridge, or Berwick Bridge, a red sandstone structure with fourteen arches, was built by James I of England, and VI of Scotland, in order to join his two kingdoms after the Union of the Crowns in 1603.

1633. Charles 1 visited Berwick.

1639. The army of Charles 1 opposed that of General Alexander Leslie in Berwick, in the Bishops Wars which were concerned with bringing the Presbyterian Church of Scotland under King Charles control ,where he stated that disputed questions surrounding Berwick should now be referred to another general assembly or to the Scottish Parliament.

The Treaty of Berwick (also known as the Peace of Berwick or the Pacification of Berwick) was signed on 18 June 1639 between England and Scotland. The agreement, overall, officially ended the war even though both sides saw it only as a temporary truce. After the treaty was signed, King Charles immediately began to gather the resources he needed in order to strengthen his armies. After a disastrous skirmish at Kelso, between the English advance guard and the Scottish Covenanter Army, the Earl of Holland fled back to the king's headquarters at Berwick. Along with the unsuccessful English naval campaign at Hamilton, this now meant that King Charles was forced to sign a truce. He conceded to the Scots the right to a Free Church Assembly and a free parliament. These rights were asserted (with the right to keep the existing legal structure instead of a separate parliament) along with the extension to Scotland of The Bill of Rights (which set out the conditions and powers of a monarch) in the Treaty of Union 1707, which would lead to the unification of Scotland with England and Wales.

1648. Royalists/Cavaliers, with Scottish support, seized Berwick and Carlisle, in April and so began the English Civil War.

1650. Oliver Cromwell stayed in Berwick on the 12th July, passing through on his way to the Battle of Dunbar.

1657. Oliver Cromwell, the Lord Protector, again visited Berwick.

1660. Following the accession of Charles II to the throne, Berwick welcomed the news by ringing the town bells and bonfires blazing.

1707. The Act of Union between Scotland and England. Berwick, though never formally annexed to England, always had the contentious issue about whether the town belonged to England or Scotland, which was ended in 1707 by this union.

1717-1721. The Royal Tweed Bridge was built.

1721. The Barracks were completed in response to objections from the town about billeting soldiers in public houses.

1746. The Wales and Berwick Act, since repealed, was passed to state that whenever legislation was passed referring to England, it should now include Berwick, as part of England. The Act of Union in 1707 marked the turning point for Berwick and once more trade was able to resume with Scotland's hinterland. With this resumption of trade, prosperity grew and between 1750 and 1850, considerable development took place. It was this development that gives Berwick its architectural character today. A quayside had existed in medieval times but to accommodate new trade, Little Dock was built and the quay extended in 1760. Berwick, today, still remains within the laws and legal system of England and Wales. Berwick was

Berwick

later annexed to England, and made part of that country, though there was some feeling that it was a separate entity, but this fact was never really believed properly, and was actually undone, by certain Acts.

1836. Berwick upon Tweed Municipal Borough, local government district was created/ made a county. It was abolished in 1974.

1847. The Royal Border Bridge with its impressive 720-yard-long railway viaduct with 28 arches , was built by Robert Stephenson to carry the East Coast Main Line, 126 feet above the River Tweed, between then and 1850, being opened by Queen Victoria, then, in that year.

1853. When Queen Victoria signed the declaration of war on Russia, to begin the Crimean War, she did so in name of "Victoria, Queen of Great Britain, Ireland, Berwick upon Tweed and the British domains beyond the sea !".

1856. At the Crimean War's ending, in The Treaty of Paris, Berwick was not mentioned.

Although most of Berwick Castle was demolished in the 19th century to make way for the railway, the military barracks remain, as do the town's rampart walls – one of the finest remaining examples of its type in the country. Today the ruin of Berwick Castle, originally a piece of Scotland, is a sad shell of its former strength, besieged and occupied again and again by the English until, finally, even the border was moved further into Scotland to accommodate Berwick as an "English" castle and Burgh, thereby fully denying it's Scottish roots.

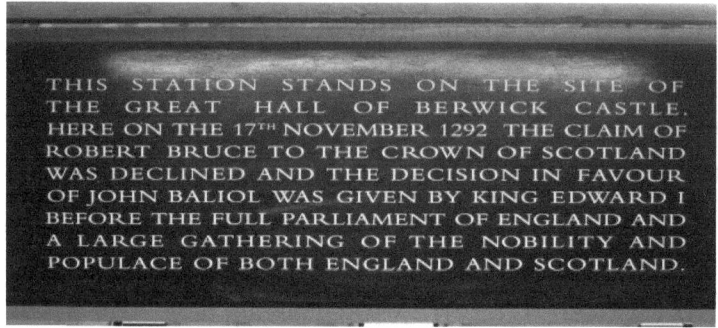

1881. From then, Berwick has remained a traditional market town and also has some notable architectural features, in particular its defence ramparts and Barrack buildings, home to the Kings Own Scottish Borderers(the KOSB) since 29th July,1881. The Regiment had been created in 1689 as a crisis measure for the defence of Edinburgh against the Jacobites. The Regiment was recruited "by beat of drum" along the Royal Mile (the High Street in the

Old Town) of the City of Edinburgh in the record time of two hours with men (over200) flocking to join the Earl of Leven to safeguard their city. In 2006 ,under changes delivered by the Government's Future Infantry Structure, the regiment became part of the Royal Regiment of Scotland ,then leaving their Berwick Barracks in November 1963.Berwick Barracks, which became the first purpose built barracks in the country, were begun in 1717, this being the last major and military project undertaken by the Crown in Berwick. Their regimental music had as as a march: 'Blue Bonnets O'er the Border', originally the march of the Scottish Borderers Militia! Their badge was the Cross of St. Andrew upon a circlet inscribed *King's Own Scottish Borderers*. Within this circlet was Edinburgh Castle with 3 turrets, each with flag flying to the left whilst, surrounding the circlet,was a wreath of thistles. The Royal Crest with St. Edward's Crown surmounted the whole.

Kevin Scott

Berwick

1885. Berwick, which had remained a county in its own right, and had not been included in Northumberland for parliamentary purposes, now officially became English.

1890. Berwick County Council was formed by the local government (Scotland) Act, 1889.

1928. The Royal Tweed Bridge, or New Bridge, was built between 1925 and 1928 and opened by HRH, Edward VIII, Prince of Wales. It has the English coat of arms on the south side of river, whilst, the Scottish arms strangely adorn its north side. I say strange, as the actual border sign is now some three miles into Scotland, from the middle of this bridge, notwithstanding the fact that news reports, from that time, referred to the bridge as it's connecting the two countries.

1928. The National Party of Scotland (later SNP) was formed. One of its founder members, one Wendy Wood, went on to great acclaim as moving the border signs to the middle of the River Tweed ,or road bridges crossing it, as a protest. She was also linked to the Society known as the Scottish Patriots, now 200 strong, a point she alludes to in her excellent autobiography entitled ,"Yours sincerely, for Scotland."

1959. Berwick Town council applied for a new coat of arms to Lord Lyon of Scotland, as the design went back to its time as one of four Royal Burghs of Scotland, and the English equivalent wouldn't help them. So too, at this time ,was there mention that the River Tweed still fell, properly, under Scots law and that Berwick has a Church of Scotland, the latter since John Knox, himself, had preached there in earlier times.

1966. In response to Queen Victoria's omission of naming Berwick in the peace treaty with Russia at the end of the Crimean War, a Pravda newspaper journalist now accepts Berwick town's mayors assurances to "please tell the Russian people that they can now sleep peacefully in their beds", as they , still technically, had been at war with the superpower!, when the Treaty of Paris was signed in 1856 to conclude the war against Russia.

1972 England is now officially defined as "subject to any alteration of boundaries under part IV of the Local Government Act, 1972.

Berwick

1973. The Queen Mother visits Berwick on St George's Day.

1974. On the 1st April, the Borough of Berwick upon Tweed was created by the merger of the previous borugh of Berwick upon Tweed with Belford, Glendale,and Norham and Islandshires Rural Districts, by a Royal charter from Queen Elizabeth II, who confirms its borough status, eventually still not to be officially amalgamated into the County of Northumberland ,until this year.

1977. Princess Anne, the Queen's daughter, visits Berwick.

1978. The Interpretation Act now provides that, in legislation passed between 1967 and 1974, " any reference to England, includes Berwick upon Tweed and Monmouthshire (Monmouthshire is now fully incorporated into Wales.)

1999. The marine boundary was controversially adjusted by the Scottish Adjacent Waters Boundaries Order 1999, so that the (Scotland/England) boundary within the territorial waters up to the 12 mile/19 km limit is 0.09 km north of the boundary, for oil installations established by the Civil Jurisdiction Offshores activities Order 1987.

2002. A Scottish Tourist Board chiefs PR stunt was attempted to buy back the town (Berwick) by offering to repay the ransom demand by the English King of England, some 840 years earlier.

2004. Berwickers turned down the opportunity of a referendum, under New Labour's idea of a Regional Assembly, to mirror the Scots and the Welsh.

2007. The Berwick Civic Society campaigned for road signs at all entrances to Berwick's old county, adding "You are now entering the Ancient County of Berwickshire.

2008. A Civil Parish and Town Council were created in 2008,the same year as the Berwick Advertiser ran a poll on just how many Berwickers would want to relocate north of the border.78% replied yes, whilst only a week later, a mock referendum was conducted in Berwick, commissioned for a UK television documentary (Tonight-ITV),under the conspicuous heading 'England v Scotland', which found that out of those who were polled, a surprising amount, 67% ,also favoured a return to Scotland. This was probably swayed by the financial lures of better Scottish healthcare, free higher education, free prescriptions, free dental and eye checkups, its legal system, as well as enjoying free university places, and better care for the elderly and public transport , all under a Scottish Parliament. As the little town of Berwick's taxes were being drained down south to London, little seemed to be coming back up.

In this respect at least, the resulting media interest placed Berwick, and its relationship to the border, in the political spotlight, as well as a poll conducted by Border TV idea backed by the leader of Borders Regional Council. As the leader of Berwick's Town Council, Elizabeth Hunter, freely admitted ; "we feel we're a bit unloved up here ,a feeling that the Scots are better off"." Some dared to report it as "an audacious land-grab"!(Hello, just read on, please)

So too, the towns Liberal Democrat MP who backed the idea of the border moving , but said that its moving would take massive negotiation and legal changes, and therefore was" not a very realistic option. Try telling that to the former East and West Germany, a slightly bigger concept, as being of too much hassle, compared with their total reunification in October 1990.

The Independent Newspaper reports on Berwick as being the most under populated part of England, as SNP MSP, Christine Grahame(now Creech) starts making calls , as does Alex Salmond, the ruling ,political party's charismatic leader, in Edinburgh's new Scottish Parliament, for Berwick to again become part of Scotland! The legal status of Berwick's dichotomy lies in the fact that the land that Berwick stands on is still, legally, part of Scotland, the town itself being a Crown dependency, like the Falkland Isles so, theoretically, an English town on Scottish soil. Confusing, it is, with two separate legal jurisdictions also covering it.

Christine Grahame: 'That the Parliament notes the referendum campaign in Berwick-upon-Tweed, 990 years after the town was ceded to Scotland following the Battle of Carham, to gauge support for the town being returned

Berwick

to the fold of Scottish nationhood; notes that Berwickers are once again considering the benefits of being part of Scotland; recognises the strong levels of support in the town for such a move, which sees the benefits that Scotland has derived from slowly removing the barriers to progress and prosperity by becoming increasingly independent of London control; agrees that we would warmly welcome Berwick-upon-Tweed back into the nation of Scotland as we move to regaining our full independence, and urges Scottish ministers to begin negotiations with HM Government to secure Berwick-upon-Tweed's restoration as part of the nation of Scotland'

To be continued...........

Kevin Scott

Governors, or Keepers, of Berwick Castle

Sir William Douglas the Hardy, 1294-1296 surrendered to Edward1 of England following the Massacre of Berwick

Sir Robert Lauder of The Bass, to circa 1330.

Robert Lauder of Edrington (later, Robert Lauder of The Bass), 1461/2-1474.

David, Earl of Crawford, 1474-1478.

Sir Robert Lauder of Edrington, Knt., 1478-1482.

Sir Patrick Hepburn, 1st Lord Hailes, 1482 (last Scottish governor).

Sir William Drury (d.1579), Marshal of Berwick-upon-Tweed, before 1564.

Francis Russell, 2nd Earl of Bedford, appointed 1564

Sir George Bowes of Streatlam, Co.Durham (d.1580), Marshal of Berwick. In 1568 he escorted Mary, Queen of Scots, from Carlisle to Bolton Castle.

***

Berwick

Who had Berwick, and when?

833. When Danish King Oseth visited, *Scottish*

973. King Edgar formally granted town to Kenneth II, *Scottish*.

1018. Still in Scots hands at Battle of Carham, *Scottish*.

1029. Danish King Canute recognises Lothian as Scottish.

1097. King Edgar gifts Berwick to St.Cuthbert, *English*.

1097. King Edgar takes Berwick back shortly after , *Scottish*.

1120. King David makes Berwick a Royal Burgh, *Scottish*.

1167. King William, "the Lion" imprisons men at Berwick, *Scottish*.

1174. King William passes town to King Henry II for 15 years, as part ransom for Wm 1 of Scotland, *English*.

1189. King Richard 1returns/ sells town back to William 1, raising money for the Crusades, *Scottish*.

1216. King John retakes from King Alexander II, *English*.

1217. King Alexander II receives Berwick back, *Scottish*.

1237. The Treaty of York confirms the border, with Berwick on the Scottish side, *Scottish*.

1296. King Edward I, the "Hammer of the Scots" brutally massacres Berwick, and all its inhabitants. *English*.

1297. English desert town and castle after defeat at the Battle of Stirling Bridge, *Scottish*.

1299. Edward II regains the town easily, *English*.

1318. Robert the Bruce takes the town, *Scottish*.

1333. King Edward III takes Berwick after Battle of Halidon Hill, *English*.

1355. William Douglas briefly takes control of Castle, *Scottish*.

1355. King Edward III regains control of Berwick, *English*.

1378. Sq Alex. Ramsay, unofficially, storms Castle, *Scottish*.

1378. The Earl of Northumberland regains Berwick only 8 days later, *English*

1383. King Richard states that Berwick "is situated beyond the limits of the kingdom," *English*.

1384. Earl Percy, bribed by Scots to give up Berwick, *Scottish*.

Berwick

1384.Earl Percy bribes back town, fearing for his life, *English*.

1403.King Harry 'Hotspur' gifts Berwick to the Scots, *Scottish*.

1405.King Henry IV captures Berwick, *English*.

1432.Berwick is declined by Scots as a bargain chip, *English*.

1461.King Henry VI gifts Berwick to Scotland for James II help in his fight against Yorkists, *Scottish*.

1482. Richard, Duke of Gloucester (future King Richard III) takes Berwick for the last conquest, *English*.

1488.King Henry VII almost cedes Berwick to King James III, in marriage truce, but backs out last minute. *English*.

About the Author

KEVIN SCOTT was born in Hawick, Scottish Borders in 1962. His grandfather played for the Hawick Rugby Club - the 'Greens' and his father turned out for Kelso RFC. His family moved to West of Scotland in 1970's but he returned to live and work in The Borders from time to time. He has relations in Peebles, Kelso, Hawick, Berwick, Swinton, and Coldstream. Kevin played competitive club rugby himself for over 20 years.

Since leaving Hutchesons' Grammar School in 1981, he has had many sales careers, including grocery (Bryant & May, Tennents Brewery), sports (Rangers FC, Gala, Selkirk & Melrose

RFC), advertising(first revolving boards in Scottish Football and first post padding advertising in Scottish Rugby) and subsequent medical roles with Abbott Labs., Nutricia and Danone.

An avid reader and writer of articles for international ex-pat communities, Kevin set up, and has run a Clan Scott Scotland group for the past 22 years. He is Secretary, Treasurer and Deputy Chairman of such with awards having been made in tribute to his enthusiasm and shared knowledge of Borders history, with the website recording 'hits' of 9 000+ .In 2018 he penned around 60+ articles, as well as editing the quarterly Bellendean Bugle editions ,sent out to Members.

A keen, and diverse, subject reader, Kevin has devised board games, written poetry and, now, with around 6 short stories, has finally succumbed to his family's wishes in publishing some of these, for hopefully, you, the reader's enjoyment.